D1682505

MANAGING
CASH FLOW

MANAGING CASH FLOW

JOHN M. KELLY

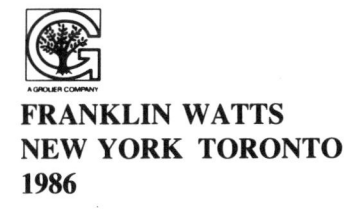

FRANKLIN WATTS
NEW YORK TORONTO
1986

Library of Congress Cataloging in Publication Data

Kelly, John M.
Managing cash flow.

Includes index.
1. Cash flow. 2. Cash management. I. Title.
HG4028.C45K453   1986   658.1'5244 86-5657
ISBN 0-531-15509-9

Copyright © 1986 by Alexander Hamilton Institute, Inc.
All rights reserved
Printed in the United States of America
5 4 3 2 1

CONTENTS

INTRODUCTION 1

1 GETTING TO KNOW CASH FLOW 3

What is cash flow? 4
Cash flow and profit 5
Cash as an asset 6
Why is cash flow important? 7
Cash consciousness 8

2 FOCUSING ON INVENTORY 11

The right level of inventory 12
Reviewing the inventory 15
Using the ABC analysis 15
The costs of carrying inventory 18
Measuring inventory turnover 21
Return on inventory investment 23

3 INVENTORY CONTROL AND REDUCTION TECHNIQUES 29

Examining product components	30
Making an EOQ analysis	32
Measuring the EOQ effect on cash flow	35
Solving an order quantity problem	37
Cutting the order cost	38
Applying EOQ to production	38

4 HOW TO HANDLE OBSOLETE AND EXCESS INVENTORY AND GUARD AGAINST THEFT 41

Days of inventory on hand	42
Generating cash from excess inventory	44
Materials requirement planning	45
Accounting for inventories	47
Inventory and security	51
How security losses hurt cash flow	51
Limiting the cash flow impact of security losses	52

5 GETTING THE MOST CASH FLOW OUT OF PURCHASE VOLUME DISCOUNTS 55

The Kraken Container Corporation	55
The break-even discount	57
The question of timing	60
Impact on cash flow	61

6 CONTROLLING ACCOUNTS RECEIVABLE — 71

Effect on cash flow — 72
Days sales outstanding — 74
Aging receivables — 76
Analyzing customer accounts — 80

7 HOW TO USE A WEIGHTED ANALYSIS TO IMPROVE CASH FLOW — 83

Dollar days outstanding — 83
Cash flow effect — 87
Isolating the variables — 89
Walton Pipe Co. — 89
Cash flow impact — 94

8 MAKING THE CREDIT DECISION AND SETTING PAYMENT TERMS — 97

Tyburn Tool, Ltd. — 98
Examining the cash flow effect — 99
Making credit decisions — 100
Credit terms and cash flow — 105
Southern Housewares, Inc. — 105
Apex Chemical Corp. — 106
Blair Manufacturing Co. — 109
Need for realistic assumptions — 110

9 HOW TO EVALUATE YOUR CUSTOMERS TO MAXIMIZE CASH FLOW — 113

The cash flow impact of credit risks	113
Timing of cash flows	115
Looking at product mix	118
Profit margins and credit policy	119
Evaluating a potential customer	122
Risk classification	124
Credit evaluation report	125

10 CASH FLOW AND CAPITAL SPENDING 129

When to use payback period	131
Applying payback analysis	132
The bailout factor	133
Depreciation and taxes	134
Using net present value	137
The present value index	138
Internal rate of return	139
Risk in capital projects	141
Identifying capital projects	144
Evaluating capital projects	146
Creative approaches to capital spending	147

11 IMPROVING CASH FLOW IN THE PRODUCTION PROCESS 151

Reviewing setup schedules	152
Production efficiency	153
Exploring production scheduling	157
Scrap and cash flow	159
Quality control	160
Conservation	162
Shipping	162
Value analysis	163
Make or buy?	165

12 IMPROVING OPERATIONS AND PROCEDURES TO CONSERVE CASH — 167

Accounting	167
Selling costs	168
Legal costs	169
Giveaways	170
Audits	171
Insurance	171
Employee relations	172
Maintenance	174
Communications	174
Clerical costs	174
Forms	175
Zero-base budgeting	176
Security	177

13 FINANCING CASH FLOWS — 179

Sales growth	179
Cash flow factors	182
Bank financing	184
Alternative financing	186
Factoring	189

14 HOW TO CONSERVE CASH THROUGH LEASING — 191

Deciding whether to lease	196
The economics of the lease or buy decision	197

APPENDIX — 203

INDEX — 207

EXHIBITS

1	The effect of a change in inventory level on cash flow	12
2	The impact on cash flow from an excessive reduction in inventory	14
3	An ABC analysis of inventory parts	17
4	Cash flow effect of reducing "A" and "C" inventory items	18
5	The effect of increased inventory turnover on cash flow	22
6	Analyzing the return on inventory investment by product	24
7	Improving return on inventory and cash flow	26
8	The economic order quantity analysis	31
9	Average inventory and costs before EOQ	33
10	Average inventory and costs after EOQ	36
11	Comparing monthly and weekly production costs	39
12	How to identify and eliminate slow-moving and obsolete inventory	43
13	Cash flow analysis of materials requirements planning (MRP)	48
14	Raw materials purchase discounts and carrying cost analysis	56
15	Break-even analysis of volume discounts	59

xi

16	Monthly cash flows with taking all volume discounts	62
17	Monthly cash flows excluding some volume discounts	64
18	Monthly cash flows excluding sheet steel discount	68
19	Cash flow effect of credit policy	73
20	Cash flow effect from $1 million in sales	75
21	Aging report on accounts receivable	78
22	Aging report on four customers	80
23	Cash flow effect of receivables on customers' accounts	82
24	Dollar days outstanding for two companies	85
25	Cash flow effect of delayed invoicing	88
26	Target versus actual accounts receivable	90
27	Analysis of variables in accounts receivable	92
28	Classifying potential customers by risk	98
29	Evaluating credit risk and cash flows	103
30	Cash flow effect of increasing credit days	107
31	Analyzing the effects of offering trade discounts	108
32	Cash flow effect of tightening credit terms	110
33	Cash flow evaluation of customers	114
34	The cash flow effect of a bad debt	115
35	The timing of cash flows on credit decisions	116
36	Effect on cash of delays in customer payments	117
37	Profit margins and cash flows	120
38	Cash flow effects of discretionary spending	123
39	Classifying customers by risk	124
40	Analysis of sales by risk class	126
41	Sample credit evaluation form	127
42	Sample credit evaluation form	128
43	Calculating internal rate of return (IRR)	140
44	Example of capital spending evaluation form	149
45	Blank form of capital spending evaluation	150
46	Cash flow effect of monthly and weekly production runs	153
47	Calculating the make/buy decision	165
48	Projected cash flow—Davis Software Corporation	180
49	Positive and negative cash flow factors	183
50	The cost of the purchase option	199
51	The cost of the lease option	200

MANAGING
CASH FLOW

INTRODUCTION

"He's never had to meet a payroll." You've heard this phrase as a description of a person who, even if he has a sound theoretical knowledge of business, hasn't been initiated into the stark realities of actually running a company.

Operating a business is more than just playing with numbers. If Friday afternoon comes along and you don't have the cash on hand to pay your employees, you are in serious trouble. The same holds true when a supplier demands payment of an invoice. Promises, expectations, hopes, and explanations are not enough. You need CASH and you need it right now, not next week, not even tomorrow.

Managing Cash Flow will alert every manager in your organization to the vital need for maintaining a healthy cash flow.

Written not for the financial specialist but for every operating manager, *Managing Cash Flow* is filled with proven techniques that will enable you to take full advantage of all your cash and avoid common cash-induced problems. It shows you how to:

- Squeeze more cash out of your accounts receivable and get your hands on it faster

- Spot those customers whose accounts are actually costing you money although they may appear to be profitable
- Cut the amount of cash you have tied up in inventories
- Transform scrap into cash
- Turn your manufacturing facilities into a "cash machine"
- Alter your operating procedures to plug cash leaks
- Obtain financing when you thought your credit was used up
- Make capital spending recommendations and decisions based on the factor that really counts—cash flow
- Expand your business without spending any cash at all

Managing Cash Flow is a book that needs to be read by every manager. The purchasing manager will find specific ways to help his company over a cash flow crisis. The production supervisor will learn how to recognize cash flow improvement opportunities all around him. The engineer, the credit supervisor, the office manager—they will all see how they can contribute to a healthier cash flow and a stronger company.

But this book is more than a compendium of proven cash flow techniques. It wakes your people up to cash consciousness. It highlights the vital difference between cash flow and profit. It graphically illustrates how even a profitable company can quickly go bankrupt if its managers ignore cash flow problems. It provides an in-depth understanding of the basic concepts of cash flow so that you can spot hundreds of potential cash flow improvement opportunities right in your own company.

More and more companies have become acutely aware that cash flow cannot be left to chance. They are looking for managers who keenly appreciate that the timing and amount of their cash flows are as crucially important as profit. This book is for every manager who realizes that the responsibility for cash flow cannot be left to someone else, and for the executive who wants to impart that idea to his staff.

Managing Cash Flow is an action book. It tells you what to do today so that you can be certain you will have the cash to meet your payroll, pay your bills, maintain your credit, and expand your business tomorrow.

1

GETTING TO KNOW CASH FLOW

How much cash does your business have? How much cash does it need? How does it generate and use its cash? How do its revenues and costs affect the cash that it has available for expansion?

These are vital questions. Without cash, companies soon cease to exist. Still, many managers are not quite sure how to measure and control the cash flowing into and out of their companies, and how that cash relates to profit. They make the decisions that affect cash flow, and yet they often leave the cash flow consequences of those decisions to the financial experts.

Historically, business performance has been evaluated principally on the concept of accrued profit. Over long periods of time, accrued profits, after adjusting for dividends and capital investments, tend to equal net cash flow.

However, profits and cash flows rarely are equal for periods of time as short as one year. Most managers must focus on producing results over one year and often shorter time periods. They may make thousands of decisions during a year in conducting the day-to-day operations of their firms.

There have been dramatic changes in recent years that now require that successful managers, whatever their area of responsibility, be acutely aware of the cash flow as well as the profit consequences of their decisions.

These changes include longer and more complex credit terms to customers, constantly changing material costs, and the substitution of highly specialized and longer-lasting plant and equipment for labor. Planning is also tending to cover longer periods of time, which is extending the business horizon.

Such changes increase the danger that the leads and lags between profit and cash flow will become longer and more pervasive. Today's managers must adjust to these changes to ensure that they do achieve their firms' long-term objectives.

WHAT IS CASH FLOW?

The movement of cash into and out of a business is known as cash flow. It has to do with the timing of cash transactions and the use of cash as an asset. Cash flow is a process, the way that a company generates and uses its cash.

Some analysts define cash flow according to the following formula:

```
  NET PROFIT
+ DEPRECIATION
− INCREASE IN ACCOUNTS RECEIVABLE
− INCREASE IN INVENTORIES
+ INCREASE IN ACCOUNTS PAYABLE
= CASH FLOW
```

You can quantify the net cash flow of a business by measuring the change in the cash balance during a given period. While the formula does not give a total picture of cash flow, it points out some of the most important elements in the process.

Clearly, profits are the major source of cash flow into a company. Depreciation, which a company's accountants subtract from earnings to recognize the gradual expenditure of the company's real assets is added back to determine cash flow because it really doesn't involve any cash expenditure. Accounts receivable increases are subtracted, although they are counted as a portion of profit, because they represent cash that the company has not yet received. Inventory increases are subtracted because they require an expenditure of cash now. Increases in accounts payable are added to cash flow, although the related costs have been recognized on the books as having been spent, because the cash has not yet left the company's treasury. (Note that if accounts receivable or inventory decrease, the amount of decrease would be added to cash flow; if accounts payable decrease, that amount would be subtracted.)

CASH FLOW AND PROFIT

A good way to appreciate the concept of cash flow is to compare it with the idea of profit. All managers understand and appreciate profit. If a company is able to manufacture an item for a total cost of $100, including overhead, and sell the same item for $120, then the firm has made a $20 profit on the transaction. But what if after buying the product the customer is slow to pay his bill? Six months pass before the account is settled. The selling company still shows a profit, but if it has bills of its own coming due during those six months, or if it wants to invest in expanded facilities, it will not have the cash on hand. So, despite its profit, the company is short of cash. It has a cash flow problem.

Profit is static. It is concerned with costs versus revenues. Cash flow, however, is dynamic. It is concerned with the movement and timing of money, cash coming in versus cash being paid out. Profit is an accounting concept. Cash flow is an operating concept.

Take the case of a jewelry store. It sells diamonds with a 100 percent markup. The store clearly makes a substantial profit on each sale. But the merchant must also have a wide variety of stones on hand. As much stock is kept in the store as is sold in an entire year. That means that the average item remains in inventory for a full year.

The store, therefore, must purchase a diamond without expecting to recoup the purchase amount until twelve months later. Since the store's own suppliers will not wait to be paid, the store must have enough cash to invest in inventories and still keep operating until sales return the cost and profit. This cash must have a source: either the original investment capital, or cash that has been accumulated from past profits, or outside financing. The cash also has a cost. What if the store borrows from a bank to finance its inventory and pays 25 percent interest? Since the average item is held for a year before being sold, the interest payment of 25 percent will eat into the markup. The profit on the sale has immediately been reduced to 75 percent of the cost because of the timing of the cash flows.

This example points out another fact about cash flow and profit: they are intimately linked.

- If cash flow is insufficient and capital has to be borrowed to maintain operations, then the interest that will have to be paid will reduce profits.
- If costs rise to the extent that a company is not making a profit, then cash flow problems are bound to arise as operations deplete cash reserves.
- If a cash shortage forces a company to curtail operations, then the total amount of profit will diminish.
- If a company uses its cash wisely, investing the surplus in interest-bearing securities or successful expansion, for example, then the cash will produce a yield which will contribute to profit.

CASH AS AN ASSET

While cash has always been important in business transactions, many companies in the past have looked on it as a neutral medium of exchange rather than as a true asset. Spurred by the rising interest rates and credit shortages of the past decades, more and more managers now see the company's cash as one of its most valuable assets.

Just as products cannot be manufactured without factories and equipment, a business cannot operate without cash. Just as a shortage of manufacturing capacity prevents an expansion of business, so a shortage of cash places limits on a company as well. And just as the investment in plant and equipment costs the company money—in terms of interest or dividend payments—but also yields profits, so does the company's cash carry a price and yield a return.

Because it is an important asset, cash must be managed as such. No company, even a highly profitable one, can operate for long if an adequate inflow of cash is not maintained. Few companies can afford to have excess cash sitting in noninterest bearing accounts any more than they can afford to have money invested in idle machinery or plants. And no company can hope to expand its business unless the availability of cash is planned just as carefully as the availability of manufacturing capacity, labor, and materials.

WHY IS CASH FLOW IMPORTANT?

Cash flow is vitally important because cash problems are the most common cause of business failures. To keep operating, a company must pay its bills. It cannot pay with future revenue, or plans, or hopes, or promises. It has to use the cash that is on hand at the moment the bill comes due. Cash that was used to purchase inventories last month, or cash that is expected from customers next month, cannot pay today's bills. If the cash is not on hand, credit may be curtailed, shipments of materials cut off, and operations immediately disrupted. Every firm that has faced the difficulty of finding the cash to make a weekly payroll knows the vital significance of healthy cash flow.

The case of W.T. Grant & Co., a major U.S. retailer, provides an example of the dangers of insufficient cash flow. Reported profits were increasing, but cash flow was decreasing and eventually turned negative. Inventories ballooned. Local managers and buyers continued to operate as usual. As a result, Grant began to have trouble paying its bills. By the time the cash crisis hit, few options were open. Cash flow imbalances were one of the important factors in driving this huge retailer into bankruptcy and eventual liquidation.

Cash flow problems are not limited to ailing or unprofitable firms. Consider, for example, a successful Texas company which made tools for oil exploration. The company had developed a major new product which it thought would be popular with the drilling firms which were its customers. It spent cash on research and development, expansion of its facilities, new machinery, and additional marketing efforts.

However, the product's introduction coincided with a six-month slump in the oil drilling industry. The firm's customers, though interested in the new product, delayed their purchases. As a result, the company's cash outflows were not matched by inflows. Its cash reserves were quickly depleted. It had to delay paying some of its bills. This damaged its credit rating. Workers were laid off and operations curtailed. Although the company survived, the cash flow crisis was harrowing.

This company's problems had little to do with profitability. It made a healthy profit on all of its sales. What happened was that the timing of cash receipts and expenditures did not mesh. The company had a cash flow problem. And given the snowball effect of the problem, continuation of business as usual could have forced the company into bankruptcy.

In addition to being the lifeblood of daily operations, cash is the fuel of expansion. New products, new facilities, new equipment, acquisitions, all depend on cash flow in one of two ways. Either cash has to be accumulated from past cash flows to finance growth, or future cash flows must be sufficient to pay off the interest and principal of the loans the company uses to pay for growth. Arguing that an expansion will be profitable is not enough. Managers must demonstrate that the timing and amounts of cash that it produces will be sufficient. Bankers want to see projections of cash flow and profits. Profits are not enough.

CASH CONSCIOUSNESS

Some managers look on cash flow as an esoteric concept only of concern to the company's treasurer or controller. They understand profit and work to improve it, often because their compensation depends partly on profitability in their sector. But they look on cash flow as primarily an issue for specialists.

Throughout this book it will be shown why this attitude is wrong.

All managers are affected by cash flow issues. All managers can contribute to a healthy cash flow. But to do so, all managers must develop cash consciousness.

An example will illustrate why this is so. A company which manufactured industrial machinery was going through a period of cash scarcity. Several new product introductions had drained cash reserves but had not yet begun to yield the expected cash inflows. The company's vice-president of finance, concerned about the situation, was unpleasantly surprised to discover that expenses had shot up at the firm's plant that made exhaust fans. He immediately contacted the plant manager, who had a ready explanation.

"One of our suppliers is discontinuing a model of electric motor that we use," he said. "They wanted to clear out inventories, so they sold us a year's supply of them at 20 percent lower than the normal price."

From a profit perspective, the plant manager had acted correctly. He had obtained a major component of one of his unit's products at a significant savings. Once the fans were manufactured and sold, his division would reap a higher than normal margin of profit. What he didn't consider, however, was that by investing scarce cash in a year's inventory of the motors, he was contributing to the company's cash flow problems. If the firm had to borrow capital at 20 percent interest in order to finance the inventory, then much of the intended profit gains of buying at a lower price would be wiped out. But what if the company was not able to raise any additional cash? Immediate operating costs would still have to be met. The plant manager's action could have been the cause of a serious crisis.

CASH FLOW ALERT

The only way to develop cash consciousness in managers is to keep them informed of the company's general cash posture. Frequent memos emphasizing the need to conserve cash and to weigh the cash flow implications of all actions should be issued to all departments.

Who needs cash consciousness? Everyone in the company:

- Salesmen have to realize that just selling more is not enough. If they sell to customers who habitually pay their bills late, they are putting pressure on the company's cash flows.
- Purchasing managers must negotiate the best possible credit terms with suppliers in order to slow the outflow of funds and keep the cash position in balance.
- Credit and collection people must make sure that every effort is made to collect all of the money due the company as fast as possible.
- Production managers must wake up to the importance of the timing of cash flows—preventing delays and cutting cash-draining inefficiencies.

Once cash consciousness has been achieved throughout the company, the firm is more likely to experience not only a profitable business, but one in which a smooth flow of cash contributes to the ease and efficiency of operations and growth.

2

FOCUSING ON INVENTORY

The way you manage your inventory has a significant impact on your company's cash flow for several reasons:

- First, inventory represents a substantial investment of cash. In the average manufacturing firm it can easily represent 30 percent of total assets. Wholesale and retail firms may find that inventory represents 60 percent or more of all assets. The larger the amount and proportion of inventory to total assets, the larger the impact it has on cash flow.
- Inventory also has a substantial effect on the firm's operating cash flow cycle. The cycle is the time it takes for an investment in inventory to be recovered in cash from the sales of finished products. Accounts receivable may typically stretch out forty to sixty days. But inventory such as materials, work-in-progress, and finished products is often tied up for six months or more. The longer materials and products are in inventory, the greater the drag on cash flow.
- Lastly, inventories are an expensive and somewhat risky form of assets. Storage, handling, obsolescence, and shrinkage costs all eat into operating margins and reduce the amount of cash ulti-

mately realized from the inventory investment. Inventory must also be sold to generate cash. Selling costs and price reductions often reduce the ultimate receipts of cash.

THE RIGHT LEVEL OF INVENTORY

Generally speaking, your company's cash flow will be improved to the extent that you reduce inventory in relation to sales. Reducing inventory frees cash that can then be used for other investments or to repay loans. It also reduces the costs of maintaining stocks in reserve.

Exhibit 1 illustrates the cash flow increase from a reduction in inventory. The Ajax Tractor Co. sells 10 tractors a month at $30,000 each. A 40 percent margin results in a monthly gross profit of $120,000. Inventory is kept at 20 tractors. The 20 tractors cost $360,000 to pro-

AJAX TRACTOR CO.

	January	February	March
Sales	$ 300,000	$ 300,000	$ 300,000
Cost of sales	(180,000)	(180,000)	(180,000)
Gross profit	120,000	120,000	120,000
Inventory	360,000	270,000	270,000
Carrying cost @ 3%	(10,800)	(8,100)	(8,100)
Carrying cost reduction	—	2,700	2,700
Cash flow from inventory reduction in February	—	90,000	—
Total increase in cash flow	—	$ 92,700	$ 2,700

Exhibit 1.
The effect of a change in inventory level on cash flow

duce. Ajax's inventory carrying costs are estimated to be 3 percent per month, or $10,800.

Ajax's management decides to reduce inventory to 15 tractors in February. Ignoring other factors, Exhibit 1 shows that the inventory reduction improves cash flow by $92,700 in February and $2,700 each month thereafter.

Clearly, the maximum amount of cash flow results from holding minimal inventories. In the Ajax example, there is a onetime cash flow improvement of $90,000 in February representing the reduction in inventory, and a $2,700 cash flow improvement each month as a result of lower carrying costs.

For most companies, however, minimal inventories are not practical:

- Suppliers may be located at a considerable distance from the plant. Long lead times for ordering and receiving goods will require larger inventories.
- Substantial inventory may be tied up in work-in-progress because of the production time.
- Fluctuations in sales may require a surplus of finished goods on hand to meet peak demand.
- Customers may be very sensitive to prompt service. Companies must keep enough supplies on hand to meet their customers' needs or they might buy from other manufacturers who do maintain sufficient stocks.

The loss of a large order, or of a customer, can easily negate the cash flow improvements resulting from carrying a low inventory. Exhibit 2 illustrates this fact.

The Ajax Tractor Co. was able to improve cash flow in February by $92,700 by reducing its tractor inventory from 20 to 15. In April, however, the company sold only eight tractors, instead of the normal 10. Two sales were lost because the firm did not have the desired models in stock. As Exhibit 2 illustrates, nearly eight months' worth of carrying cost savings from lower inventory are eliminated in just one month because of the two lost tractor sales. The loss will worsen in the following months if additional sales are lost.

AJAX TRACTOR CO.

	January	February	March	April
Sales	$ 300,000	$ 300,000	$ 300,000	$ 240,000
Cost of sales	(180,000)	(180,000)	(180,000)	(144,000)
Gross profit	120,000	120,000	120,000	96,000
Inventory	360,000	270,000	270,000	270,000
Carrying cost @ 3%	(10,800)	(8,100)	(8,100)	(8,100)
Effect of inventory reduction on cash flow	—	$ 92,700	$ 2,700	$(21,300)*

*Reflects the loss of $24,000 gross profit

Exhibit 2.
The impact on cash flow from an excessive reduction in inventory

In addition, having production employees and machinery sitting idle waiting for delivery of materials because not enough are kept in stock will also have a large negative impact on cash flow.

The goal, then, is to manage your inventory, not simply to cut it to the bone. The best cash flow will result from a level of inventory which prevents excessive stock outs, allows for growth, lets you service customers in a satisfactory manner, facilitates a smooth production schedule, provides a cushion for such things as delays in delivery of strategic materials and products which do not contribute to these objectives.

Effective inventory management, therefore, requires an in-depth analysis of your own company, your market, your suppliers, and the actual business environment you face. You must design an inventory strategy that is right for your company. What works for one company may not work for another, even in the same industry. And the right inventory levels for your firm when interest rates are 7 percent will not necessarily be right when they are 17 percent. Cut inventories yes, but cut them to optimum, not minimum, levels.

REVIEWING THE INVENTORY

Every company analyzes inventories at regular intervals, usually yearly. This is a necessary means for controlling inventory levels and for comparing like periods from year to year. You should not, however, forget about inventory between specific reporting periods or physical counts. Regular inventory reviews, even if highly informal, can spot points where inventory excesses are crimping cash flow before the problem becomes severe. Here are five recommended procedures for such a review.

1. Make up a list of your top ten inventory items in terms of value and trace them through your facility, from receiving dock to the shipping of the end product. Look for bottlenecks and stockpiles.
2. Use these items to make up a "Least Wanted" list. Ask all employees for suggestions about reducing inventories of these expensive items.
3. Review open orders to spot-check for potential inventory excesses developing in the coming month. Adjust orders or delivery schedules accordingly.
4. Do a "dust check" in stock storage areas to spot those items that are literally collecting dust. Can they be scrapped? Reworked? Returned to the vendor? Made to order rather than stocked?
5. Walk through the production area and look for employees who are hoarding parts and components. Would stricter stock control or a more efficient in-plant delivery system improve this situation?

USING THE ABC ANALYSIS

Every company has only limited resources to devote to any task. For this reason, inventory management efforts should focus on the areas where they will have the greatest cash flow impact. This can be accomplished through an ABC analysis.

The concept of the ABC analysis is an application of Pareto's law, which states that in many situations a small proportion of input accounts for a large proportion of output. This is also known as the 20/80 rule. Applied to inventory, 20 percent of inventory items represents 80 percent of total value.

To do an ABC analysis:

1. List every item in your inventory. Include raw materials, maintenance and utility items, everything.
2. Multiply the average annual use of each item by the cost per unit. For example, a rubber bushing costs $0.08 per unit. You use 100,000 of them each year. The use value is $8,000.
3. List all items in descending order of use value.
4. Add the use value of all the items to find the total.
5. Go back to the top of the list and begin to add again. Stop when you reach a cumulative figure equal to 80 percent of the total. These are your A inventory items.
6. Start adding again and continue until you reach another 15 percent of the total. These are your B items.
7. The remaining items are your C category. As a rule, they represent only 5 percent of the total use value.

You will most likely find that less than a quarter of all the items are in the A category. They may include expensive components, precious metals, or basic, high-volume materials. Exhibit 3 gives an ABC analysis for the inventory of the Johnson Brothers Company, which produces lamps. The company is not real, but the analysis is typical of a real inventory.

The ABC analysis tells you nothing about correct inventory levels. Rather, it directs your attention to the inventory items which potentially represent the largest part of your inventory investment and thus have the biggest impact on your cash flow. These are the A and B items. It also lets you know which items you can safely ignore because of their inconsequential effect on cash flow—the C items.

THE JOHNSON BROTHERS COMPANY

Inventory Item	Number of Units Used Annually	Value Per Unit	Use Value	Cumulative Use Value
Category A				
Glass decoration	10,000	$ 4.00	$40,000	
Fixtures	12,000	1.50	18,000	
Brass pipe	800	17.50	14,000	
Switches	10,000	.80	8,000	
				$ 80,000
Category B				
Wire	500	12.00	6,000	
Sheet steel	2,500	1.60	4,000	
Plastic	600	5.00	3,000	
Plugs	10,000	.20	2,000	
				15,000
Category C				
Brackets	20,000	.07	1,400	
Connectors	10,000	.08	800	
Boxes	8,000	.875	700	
Bushings	5,000	.12	600	
Bolts	20,000	.02	400	
Felt	75	4.00	300	
Spacers	20,000	.01	200	
Screw #1	5,000	.02	100	
Screw #2	5,000	.02	100	
Solder	20	5.00	100	
Washers	10,000	.01	100	
				5,000
		TOTAL USE VALUE		$100,000

Exhibit 3.
An ABC analysis of inventory parts

THE JOHNSON BROTHERS COMPANY

	A Item: Fixtures	C Item: Spacers
Annual use	12,000	20,000
Cost/unit	$ 1.50	$0.01
Value of inventory	$9,000	$100
One year's carrying cost @ 30%	$2,700	$ 30
Cash flow increase from 10% inventory reduction	$270.00	$3.00

Exhibit 4.
Cash flow effect of reducing A and C inventory items

Exhibit 4 illustrates the cash flow results of inventory management as applied to the Johnson Brothers' A and C inventory items. The analysis shows why "across-the-board" inventory reductions are not necessarily an efficient use of management time and energy. The disproportionately larger effect of reducing A inventories indicates that the greatest cash flow benefits will come from focusing your attention on these items.

It is worth remembering that all inventory can be better managed when it is broken into discrete components. An ABC analysis is the best way to do this. Look at your inventory by product line, by lead time of delivery, by market. All of these divisions will help you to focus your efforts more effectively than just looking at and working with your company's aggregate inventory amount.

THE COSTS OF CARRYING INVENTORY

Inventories require a cash investment and incur carrying costs. If capital did not have to be invested to purchase or process materials, if warehouse space were free and no handling charges were incurred, a company could maintain high inventory levels without any influence on cash flow. But this is not the case. An understanding of the nature of carrying costs is important in successfully managing inventory.

A recent survey by *Purchasing* magazine estimated that total costs in the U.S. for carrying $1 of inventory for one year averaged 27¢. For fast-moving, easily handled items, the yearly carrying costs were about 15¢ for each dollar of inventory. For slow-moving, bulky items, they could be as high as 40¢.

These figures are averages representing many companies and industries. Determining your own company's carrying costs will require a detailed look at these factors. Even averages from your own industry may not reflect your own situation. The size of your company, its location relative to customers and suppliers, energy costs, and inventory strategy will affect the level of your carrying costs.

Examine the costs of two nearly identical companies. Each decides to build a new warehouse to store inventories needed to service a sales increase. One company has low debt and excellent credit. It borrows the construction funds at a 10 percent rate of interest. The other has used up its bank credit and has to turn to collateral financing which costs 18 percent. The second company will have to pay 8¢ more each year to carry each additional $1 of inventory in its new warehouse.

Below are a list of factors you should take into consideration when determining the carrying costs of inventory:

> *Cost of capital.* Some firms use the marginal interest rate on borrowings. Others calculate the figure according to the return on investment they would require from an alternative investment. But a cost somewhat higher than the cost of money in the money market or through secured loans should be used to make up for the fact that an investment in inventory entails a fair amount of risk. How much more? Five percentage points will not be an unreasonable amount to add to interest costs to reflect a normal amount of risk. If there is a relatively high risk for some products, then add a higher premium or cost to the interest portion of the carrying cost.

Storage. The cost of renting a warehouse or the cost of building your next warehouse divided by its capacity. Don't make the mistake of viewing warehouse space as "free" simply because you currently have excess warehouse capacity. Add to this figure the cost to heat, light, cool, or otherwise maintain the storage space.

Handling. Include labor charges for moving, regulating, and guarding inventory, as well as the cost and maintenance fees applicable to materials handling equipment.

Insurance. The cost of the portion of total coverage that is applicable to inventory.

Obsolescence. This results from scrapping slow-moving items or selling them at a reduced price. It can be very high for perishable or fashion items.

Damage. Through deterioration or the handling of stocks.

Shrinkage. Theft and pilferage represent substantial inventory carrying costs for many firms.

Calculate each of these components separately as they apply to particular segments of your inventory. Determine the carrying cost as an annual percentage of the value of the unit of inventory. The total of all the components should fairly represent the cost of carrying that category or segment of inventory.

You will have to use your company's experience in such areas as spoilage, shrinkage, damage, and obsolescence. Examine company reports and the results of physical inventories which identify such costs.

For a typical U.S. manufacturer's inventory, the breakdown today might look like this:

Spoilage and theft	2%
Obsolescence	3
Storage and insurance	7
Financing cost	16
Total	28%

If you do not have sufficient records to calculate component costs, you will have to use your best estimate, but remember, the carrying costs are normally quite high and surprise many managers.

When considering carrying costs, segregate the fixed and variable costs. For example, you might have to heat an entire warehouse even though the inventory level is reduced by half. Thus, heating is a fixed cost in this case. Insurance fees may not vary directly with the level of inventory kept on hand. Financing costs are variable, which is usually true for obsolescence. Having a fixed and variable cost breakdown will enable you to better assess cost savings and thus the cash flow results from managing your inventory investment.

MEASURING INVENTORY TURNOVER

Several ratios are useful in weighing the cash flow implications of inventory management. The first is turnover, the average annual cost of goods sold divided by the average inventory level.

The faster you "turn" your inventory, the lower the level of inventory you will need to support a given level of sales. Carrying costs in relation to sales will decrease.

As illustrated in Exhibit 5, initial cash flow gains are likely to be large, later gains small.

Exhibit 5 shows that if sales remain constant, all increase in inventory turnover will decrease inventory carrying costs and thus improve cash flow. The chart assumes that the annual cost of goods sold equals $5,000,000 and that inventory carrying costs average 30 percent of the value of inventory.

Remember, however, that the savings from increasing turnover do not diminish in a straight line. To improve inventory turns from one to four per year results in a 75 percent reduction in inventory carrying costs and a $1,125,000 improvement in cash flow if sales are unchanged. Improving turns from eight to twelve times, however, represents only a 33 percent saving in carrying costs and a cash flow improvement of $63,000. This assumes all carrying costs are variable.

Just as your ABC analysis tells you to focus your inventory management efforts on items with high annual use value, the chart in Exhibit 5 tells you to direct your attention to the items having the lowest turnover rates.

Inventory Turns	Average Inventory Level (000)	Annual Carrying Cost (000)	Incremental Cash Flow (000)
0.5	$10,000	$3,000	—
1	5,000	1,500	$1,500
2	2,500	750	750
3	1,667	500	250
4	1,250	375	125
5	1,000	300	75
6	833	250	50
7	714	214	36
8	625	188	26
9	556	167	21
10	500	150	17
11	455	136	14
12	416	125	11

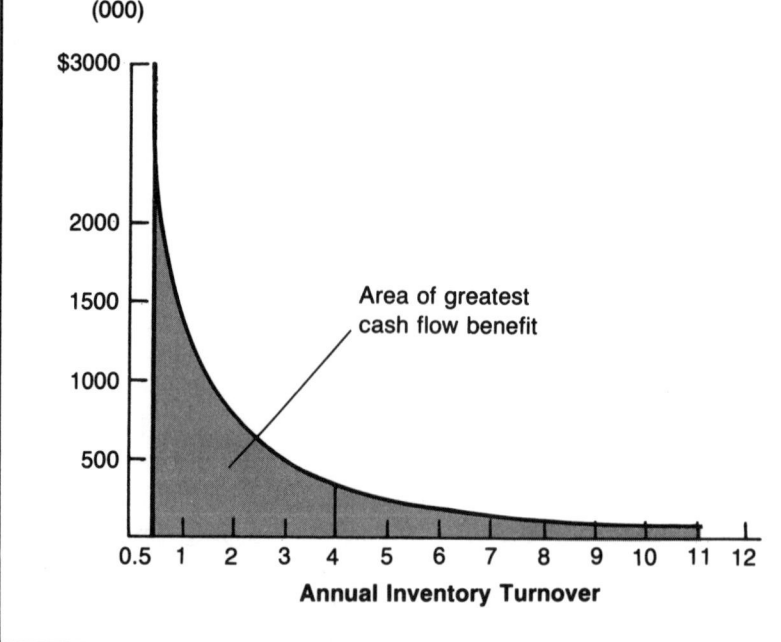

Exhibit 5.
The effect of increased inventory turnover on cash flow

RETURN ON INVENTORY INVESTMENT

Another way to use the turnover ratio to improve cash flow is to look at inventory as the investment it is. For example, a company might decide that it wishes to achieve a 40 percent return in terms of gross margin on each dollar invested in inventory.

This analysis works particularly well for finished goods inventory. Begin by preparing a chart which plots the gross margin of each product against its inventory turnover rate as shown in Exhibit 6.

The return on inventory investment equals the gross margin multiplied by the annual inventory turnover into sales. Note that the turnover for this measure is into sales, not cost of goods sold. For example, if the gross margin for an item is 25 percent and inventory turnover into sales is two times a year, the return on the inventory investment equals 50 percent.

The chart in Exhibit 6 shows various inventory items in an electronics manufacturing company. A curve which represents the desired 40 percent return is plotted. You plot the curve by dividing 40 percent by the various turnover rates. For example, 40 percent divided by 0.5 equals an 80 percent gross margin requirement for that turnover amount. Six different products are then positioned on the chart according to their actual gross profit margins and inventory turns.

Product No. 1 is a robotic control unit. While it is a slow-moving item with only one turnover of inventory a year, it is also a high-margin item. The 50 percent return on inventory puts it above the firm's 40 percent objective as indicated by the curve.

Product No. 2 is a circuit board. Though it is a relatively low-margin item, grossing only 20 percent profit, inventories are also low relative to sales, and turnover is three times a year. Its return is, therefore, acceptable.

Product No. 3 is a testing device. With a turnover of once a year for inventory, and a gross margin of 30 percent, its ROI is below the acceptable limit. The same holds true for product No. 4, a semiconductor chip; product No. 5, a rectifier; and product No. 6, a resistor.

The ROI analysis not only alerts you to products which fail to achieve acceptable levels of return on the inventory investment, it also points to the two strategies available to improve an item's cash flow.

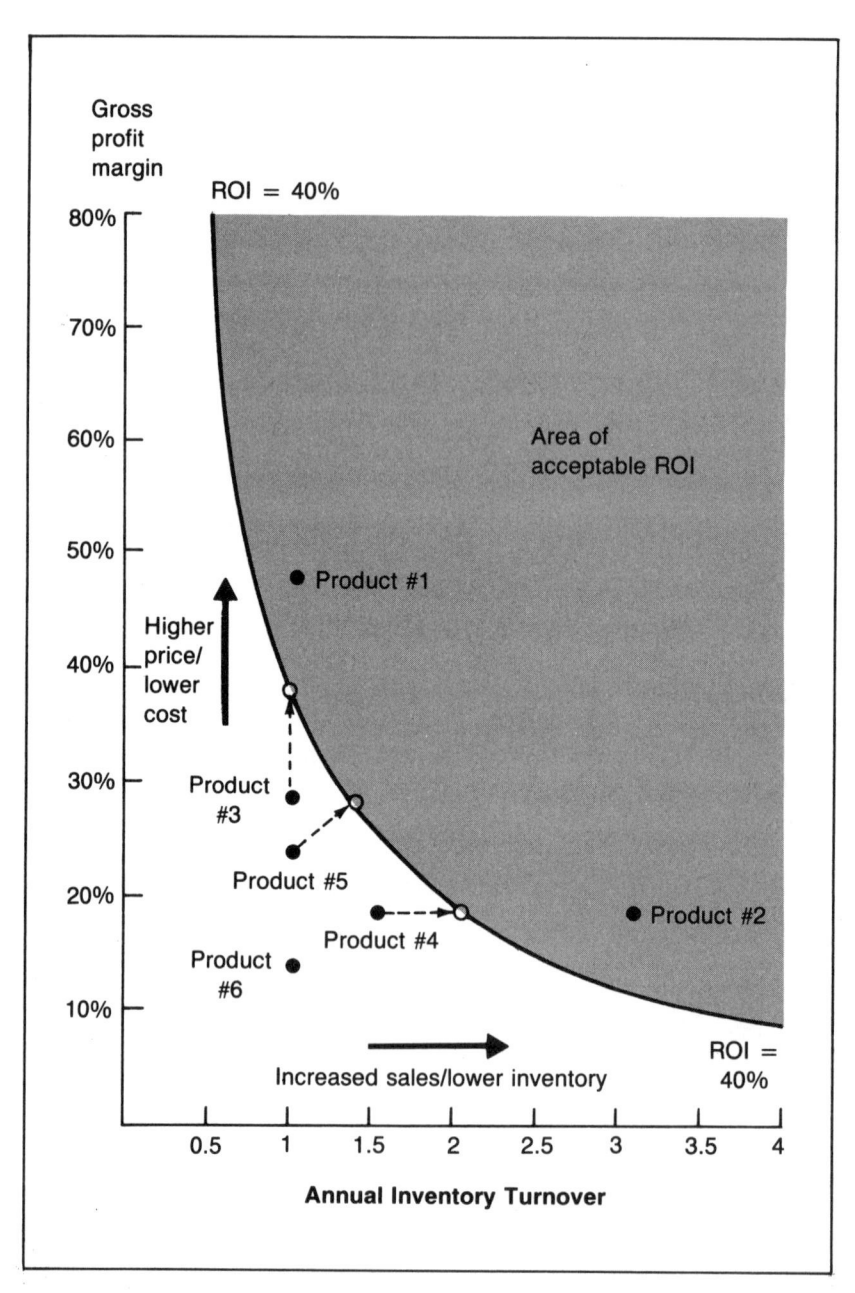

Exhibit 6.
Analyzing the return on inventory investment by product

The first strategy is to move the item to the right on the chart by either lowering inventory levels or increasing sales. The second is to move the item upward on the chart by either raising its price or cutting the cost to produce or buy it.

A combination of these two strategies is often called for. In fact, the shortest line from the product's current position to the level of acceptable ROI may indicate the most feasible combination of inventory control and margin enhancement. Product No. 5, for example, would benefit by an increase in turnover *and* margin improvement, and it might be possible to achieve the objective by improving both by relatively modest amounts rather than improving only one factor by a relatively large amount.

Exhibit 7 shows how the managers of inventory control and sales of the electronics company used this technique in relation to the four products which showed an inadequate return on inventory investment.

In the case of product No. 3, a price increase and accompanying reduction in costs raised the item's gross margin from 30 percent to 40 percent. Inventory turnover increased slightly, and the ROI improved. The annual cash flow improvement was $12,000 as shown at the bottom of Exhibit 7.

For product No. 4, increased sales and more strictly managed inventories resulted in an increase in turnover from 1.5x to 2x. This also brought the ROI to an acceptable level and improved the annual cash flow by $7,000 in addition to a onetime improvement of $10,000 represented by the inventory reduction.

A combination of strategies was used for product No. 5. Cutting costs improved the gross margin from 25 to 30 percent, while reducing inventory by $25,000 led to a higher turnover. These actions brought the product's ROI into the desired range of acceptability. The annual cash flow improvement amounted to $12,500. The inventory reduction contributed a onetime cash flow of $25,000.

Product No. 6 (not shown in Exhibit 7) had to be manufactured in bulk for production efficiency reasons. This meant a high average inventory. Sales were sluggish. Turnover could not be improved. Because of market competition, a price increase was not feasible. As a

	Product No. 3—Test Device	Product No. 4—Semiconductor	Product No. 5—Rectifier
Yearly sales	$80,000	$120,000	$100,000
Cost of sales	56,000	96,000	75,000
Gross margin	24,000	24,000	25,000
Gross margin %	30%	20%	25%
Average inventory	$80,000	$80,000	$100,000
Inventory turnover (into sales)	1x	1.5x	1x
Inventory ROI	30%	30%	25%
Target ROI	40%	40%	40%
Action:	Raise Price; Cut Cost of Sales	Increase Sales; Cut Inventory	Cut Cost of Sales; Reduce Inventory
Yearly sales	$90,000	$140,000	$100,000
Cost of sales	54,000	112,000	70,000
Gross margin	36,000	28,000	30,000
Gross margin %	40%	20%	30%
Average inventory	$80,000	$70,000	$75,000
Inventory turnover (into sales)	1.125x	2x	1.333x
New ROI	45%	40%	40%
Annual Cash Flow Improvement:			
From gross margin	$12,000	$4,000	$5,000
From carrying costs (30%)	—	3,000	7,500
Total	$12,000	$7,000	$12,500
One-time cash flow	$ —	$10,000	$25,000

Exhibit 7.
Improving return on inventory and cash flow

result, management decided to drop the product in order to eliminate its negative effect on cash flow in spite of the fact that it was marginally profitable.

CASH FLOW ALERT

Accurate physical counts are needed to properly control inventory for optimum cash flow. Ask yourself some questions: Are counts now entrusted to the least competent employees? Are employees allowed to count inventories over which they have direct authority? Is any systematic effort made to avoid errors? For example, a computerized part-numbering system can screen numbers automatically. Under this scheme, the last digit is a check. It represents the sum of the preceding digits. Incorrect numbers are spotted and flagged by the computer.

3

INVENTORY CONTROL AND REDUCTION TECHNIQUES

Economic order quantity (EOQ) is an analytical tool that tells purchasing agents how much to order and how often to order purchased parts and raw materials. It is also useful for production managers for determining the quantity of certain production activities. EOQ is a proven technique for improving cash flow.

Each purchase order involves a cost. For example:

- The cost of clerical work to prepare it
- The cost of management time to review and approve the requisition
- The cost of the accountant's time to record the transaction
- The cost to receive and inspect the shipment when it arrives
- The cost of processing the resulting invoice
- The cost of the check used to pay for the shipment.

These costs are incurred every time a separate order is placed. Collectively, they make up the order cost.

If inventories are reduced by placing more frequent orders, a point will be reached at which the improved cash flow from lower inventory carrying costs will begin to diminish because of the increase in ordering costs. The total cost of carrying and ordering inventory is lowest when these two components are equal. This cost relationship is illustrated graphically in Exhibit 8.

The table in the upper half of Exhibit 8 shows that by placing an order for 5,000 transformers 10 times a year, the cost of ordering is $1,000 ($100 × 10) which is equal to the cost of carrying the transformer inventory ($2,500 × 0.40). The total cost of $2,000, which is the sum of the ordering and the carrying cost, is lowest at this 5,000 order quantity. If the order quantity is either reduced or increased, the total inventory cost will increase.

The bottom portion of Exhibit 8 illustrates the principle graphically. The EOQ is found on the horizontal axis at the point where the total cost line is lowest. The graph also illustrates the relationship between ordering costs and carrying costs. For example, the ordering cost drops very sharply initially as the number of orders decreases, but then it starts to flatten out. The inventory carrying cost, however, increases at a constant rate over all quantities as shown by the straight line. It is affected only by the value of the inventory. The higher the inventory, the higher the carrying cost.

An EOQ analysis determines this point of lowest total cost. It therefore points toward the optimum purchasing strategy for maximizing cash flow.

EXAMINING PRODUCT COMPONENTS

The Dynalectric Communication Corporation planned a review of inventory levels of the components of one of its major products, a microwave transmission monitor. First, an ABC analysis focused management's attention on four components in category A. Each was a purchased unit. Together they represented a substantial portion of the cost of the product.

The table on the following page shows that Dynalectric spent $100,000 annually to purchase each of the components. But the inventory carrying cost and order cost were different in each case.

The ordering cost for the transformer was high because of the large amount of paperwork involved in an order, the need to review orders

ECONOMIC ORDER QUANTITY ANALYSIS

- Annual use of item   50,000 units
- Unit cost $1.00
- Total use value per year $50,000
- Order cost per order $100
- Inventory carrying cost rate 40%

Quantity per Order	Orders per Year	Order Cost	Average Inventory	Inventory Carrying Cost	Total Cost
1,000	50	$5,000	500	$ 200	$5,200
2,000	25	2,500	1,000	400	2,900
3,000	16.7	1,667	1,500	450	2,117
4,000	12.5	1,250	2,000	800	2,050
5,000	10	1,000	2,500	1,000	2,000
6,000	8.3	833	3,000	1,200	2,033
7,000	7.1	714	3,500	1,400	2,114
8,000	6.3	625	4,000	1,600	2,225
10,000	5	500	5,000	2,000	2,500

Exhibit 8.
The economic order quantity analysis

by senior engineers, and the cost of checking and handling each individual shipment. The inventory carrying cost was high because, in addition to the cost of capital invested in the inventory, the transformers required a great deal of space to store and a considerable amount of internal handling.

As with the transformer, the microprocessor's cost to place an order was high. But because of the minimal room taken up by the item in storage, the inventory carrying cost was lower.

Because of product standardization and an arrangement with the supplier, the cost to order the cathode ray tube was relatively low. But the CRT inventory was expensive to carry because of its bulk and the frequent instances of damage to components.

Transistor ordering costs were in line with those of the CRT. Inventory carrying costs were low because the items took up little space and were subject to a low rate of spoilage.

Component	Annual Use (Units)	Unit Value	Total Use Value	Cost Per Order	Inventory Carrying Cost Rate
Transformer	200	$500	$100,000	$150	40%
Microprocessor	2,222	45	100,000	150	20%
Cathode ray tube	1,000	100	100,000	25	40%
Transistor	10,000	10	100,000	25	20%

MAKING AN EOQ ANALYSIS

Exhibit 9 illustrates Dynalectric's purchasing strategy for the components, ignoring the impact of safety stocks. The order quantities have been determined rather arbitrarily. The average inventory on hand ranged from a little over a week's worth for the microprocessor to a month's worth for the transistor.

The total cost to both order and maintain inventories of all four components amounted to $11,268 per year. This cost was a direct drain

Component	Quantity Per Order	Orders Per Year	Order Cost	Average Inventory	Inventory Carrying Cost	Total Cost
Transformer	42	12	$1,800	$ 4,167	$1,667 (40%)	$ 3,467
Microprocessor	93	24	3,600	2,083	417 (20%)	4,017
Cathode ray tube	83	12	300	4,167	1,667 (40%)	1,967
Transistor	1,667	6	150	8,333	1,667 (20%)	1,817
TOTAL				$18,750		$11,268

Exhibit 9.
Average inventory and costs before EOQ

on the firm's cash flow. In addition, Dynalectric had $18,750 tied up in the average inventory.

The most convenient form of the EOQ equation for cash flow analysis is that which indicates the number of orders to place in a given time period—in this case, one year. Orders per year are then equal to inventory turns.

This version of the EOQ formula uses the following factors:

A. the requirement for the component or material during the period, expressed in monetary terms
C. the carrying cost rate for inventory expressed in decimal form as a percent of the inventory value
K. the cost of placing a single order
N. the number of orders placed during the period.

As illustrated in Exhibit 8, the lowest total cost occurs when carrying costs and order costs are equal.

Order cost equals number of orders times cost per order (NK).
Average inventory equals half the quantity of each order (½A/N).
Carrying cost equals average inventory times the carrying cost rate (C½A/N).
The ideal situation, then, is NK = C½A/N.
Solving for N, the formula becomes

$$N = \sqrt{\frac{CA}{2K}}.$$

When the solution is found, N is rounded off. A further calculation can easily determine the dollar amount of each order (A/N) and the quantity of each order (A/N divided by the unit price).

The application of this formula to the four components analyzed by Dynalectric yielded the results below. The EOQ analysis indicates the need for a number of changes in purchasing strategy.

Transformer $\quad N = \sqrt{\frac{.40(100,000)}{2(150)}} = 11.5$

INVENTORY CONTROL AND REDUCTION TECHNIQUES

Microprocessor $\quad N = \sqrt{\dfrac{.20(100{,}000)}{2(150)}} = 8.2$

Cathode ray tube $\quad N = \sqrt{\dfrac{.40(100{,}000)}{2(25)}} = 28.3$

Transistor $\quad N = \sqrt{\dfrac{.20(100{,}000)}{2(25)}} = 20.0$

The EOQ orders are rounded and compare as follows to the current ordering policy:

Product	Current annual number of orders	EOQ annual number of orders
Transformer	12	12
Microprocessor	24	8
Cathode ray tube	12	28
Transistor	6	20

In the case of the transformer, current frequency of orders and current inventory are about right; no change is needed.

For the microprocessor, however, the orders should be lower and the inventory should be increased. Because of the high cost to order and the low carrying cost, the current frequent number of orders is not economical. The company should order about $12,500 worth of the component 8 times a year ($100,000 ÷ 8).

The order frequency for both the CRT and the transistor should be increased. The lower cost of ordering these components means that orders can be placed much more frequently before ordering costs become prohibitive.

MEASURING THE EOQ EFFECT ON CASH FLOW

Dynalectric's purchasing manager then calculated the effect on cash flow if purchases were made according to the EOQ guidelines. The results are shown in Exhibit 10.

Component	Quantity Per Order	Orders Per Year	Order Cost	Average Inventory	Inventory Carrying Cost	Total Cost
Transformer	42	12	$1,800	$ 4,167	$1,667	$3,467
Microprocessor	278	8	1,200	6,250	1,250	2,450
Cathode ray tube	36	28	700	1,786	714	1,414
Transistor	500	20	500	2,500	500	1,000
TOTAL				$14,703		$8,331

Exhibit 10.
Average inventory and costs after EOQ

INVENTORY CONTROL AND REDUCTION TECHNIQUES

Comparing these amounts to those in Exhibit 9, you can see that the cash flow will be increased by $2,937 after adopting the EOQ's. This represents a 26 percent cut in total ordering and carrying costs.

In this example, the new purchasing strategy result in a 22 percent decline in average inventory levels for the four components, which generates an additional $4,047 in cash.

	Current Average Inventory	EOQ Average Inventory
Transformer	$ 4,167	$ 4,167
Microprocessor	2,083	6,250
Cathode ray tube	4,167	1,786
Transistor	8,333	2,500
Total	$18,750	$14,703

SOLVING AN ORDER QUANTITY PROBLEM

The purchasing manager runs into a common problem when he implements this change in purchasing quantities. The manufacturer of the transistor indicates that any order under 1,000 units will be charged a 2 percent premium because of the need to adjust the packaging.

To evaluate this situation, turn back to Exhibit 8. Note that while the total costs are lowest when the order quantity is 5,000 units, there is a range—from 3,200 to 8,000 units—in which the total costs do not surpass the ideal cost by more than $250. This minimal cost variation leads some analysts to think of EOQ as a range rather than a specific quantity. Within this range, the purchasing manager can select an order quantity which seems preferable in terms of shipping or packing convenience without greatly affecting the cash flow.

His additional calculations reveal that ordering 1,000 transistors ten times a year results in order costs of $1,000 and inventory carrying costs of $250, for a total of $1,250. While this is $250 greater than the ideal cost if only 500 are ordered at a time, it avoids a $2,000 price premium and it enhances the firm's cash flow.

CUTTING THE ORDER COST

In reviewing the analysis after implementing the purchasing changes, Dynalectric's managers note that the transformer is now the component with the greatest negative impact on cash flow. Still looking for improvements, they institute a program to cut the cost of ordering transformers. By standardizing the units employed in the product and by simplifying the requisition procedure for the transformer, they are able to trim the order costs from $150 to $60 per order.

A second EOQ analysis is now done on the transformer. The result indicates that it will be most economical to order 28 transformers at a time 18 times a year. This will result in an order cost of $1,080 (18 × $60) and an inventory carrying cost of $1,111 ($2,778 × 0.40). The total, $2,191 is considerably lower than the current total of $3,467. The company therefore achieves an annual cash flow increase of $1,276 on this product by simply lowering the cost of ordering a component. There is also a onetime cash flow of $1,389 from reducing the average inventory from $4,167 to $2,778.

APPLYING EOQ TO PRODUCTION

It is also possible to apply the EOQ technique to certain production activities such as machine setup time to minimize total cost and improve cash flow.

Dynalectric, for instance, produces a voltage monitor with an annual sales volume of 120,000 units. The monitor sells for $400, and production costs total $300. The company's production schedule is one production run per month. The setup costs average $1,000 per run. Each run totals 10,000 units.

	Monthly Production	Weekly Production
Total units for year	120,000	120,000
Production setups per year	12	52
Setup cost per run	$ 1,000	$ 1,000
Total setup cost	$ 12,000	$ 52,000
Production lot size (units)	10,000	2,308
Average inventory (units)	5,000	1,154
Safety stock (units)	1,000	250
Total average inventory (units)	6,000	1,404
Inventory cost per unit	$ 300	$ 300
Total average value	$1,800,000	$421,000
Annual carrying cost @ 30%	$540,000	$126,000
Total setup and carrying cost	$552,000	$178,000

Exhibit 11.
Comparing monthly and weekly production costs

In addition to the production run, Dynalectric keeps a safety stock of 1,000 units in the event sales should increase suddenly or there should be a disruption in production. Given the current inventory and production policy, therefore, the firm incurs total inventory costs of $552,000, as shown in Exhibit 11 in the monthly production column.

If production changes from monthly to weekly, setup costs for the year will increase from $12,000 to $52,000, *but* average inventory will drop dramatically from $1,800,000 to $421,000 for a substantial onetime cash flow improvement of $1,379,000. In addition, the total setup and carrying costs will decline from $552,000 to $178,000 for a cash flow improvement of $374,000 per year.

CASH FLOW ALERT

The cash flow of many firms is significantly reduced because of a boom-and-bust inventory policy. When business is booming, these companies overstock on optimistic sales forecasts. When business slows down, they are stuck with unwanted inventories. What's more, these firms end up buying in a tight market, when prices are high, and selling in a slack market, often at a reduced price. More and more firms are realizing that tightly controlled, stable inventory levels at all times are better than the radical swings of the boom-and-bust approach. Would such a policy improve cash flow at your company?

4

HOW TO HANDLE OBSOLETE AND EXCESS INVENTORY AND GUARD AGAINST THEFT

While they incur the same capital and storage costs as other inventory, slow-moving and obsolete inventories represent a serious drag on cash flow because they are likely to result in the least amount of cash when ultimately liquidated.

A good way to identify these items is to use the months-of-inventory-on-hand ratio. You can calculate it by dividing the past year's usage of the item by 12, then dividing that figure into the quantity of inventory currently on hand.

$$\frac{\text{Current inventory}}{\text{Year's use}/12} = \text{Months on hand}$$

Once you calculate the ratio for a group of inventory items, list them along with the value of the current inventory of each. From this list, derive an action list. This will include all items for which there is more than a certain number of months' stock on hand and for which the inventory represents more than a specified value. You must determine the months' stock and value limits.

Develop a specific recommendation for action for each item on the list. An item may be scrapped, reworked, or returned to the vendor in order to salvage some cash from it, or it may be retained in stock if that is considered to be the appropriate course. Normally, the sales, production, finance, and other managers work together to decide on the appropriate action. To ensure that action is taken, periodic meetings are held to review items on the action list. It requires action for the inventory items on the list to improve cash flow.

Exhibit 12 shows the analysis of a segment of inventory in a company making automobile carburetors and the appropriate action to be taken on the problem items.

DAYS OF INVENTORY ON HAND

Another way to look at inventory levels for cash flow purposes is in terms of days of inventory on hand. This ratio is derived by dividing the annual cost of sales by 360, then dividing this figure into the value of current inventory.

$$\frac{\text{Current inventory}}{\text{Annual cost of sales}/360} = \text{Days on hand}$$

All inventory contains a certain percentage of safety stock. This is material not expected to be used or sold during the period before the next delivery or production run but is kept in stock in case deliveries are late or sales increase unexpectedly. But excess safety stock reduces cash flow.

Consider a company which distributes transformers. Sales of a particular model last year cost $120,000. Deliveries from the manufacturer are made every two months. The longest delay in a delivery during the past two years was three weeks. Monthly cost of sales during the past year has never varied more than 10 percent from the average of $10,000. Current inventory is worth $60,000.

The days of inventory which are on hand total 180 days [$60,000/($120,000/360)]. That represents 120 days of safety stock beyond the maximum 60 days of inventory the company can expect to sell before the next delivery. Yet delivery delays based on two years of experience can only be expected to account for 21 days of inventory, and sales variations for 6 days (10 percent of 60 days). Even allowing a more conservative estimate for contingencies, the com-

INITIAL INVENTORY LIST

Part	Inventory on Hand in Units	Monthly Use in Units	Stock on Hand (Months)	Value
Metering rod M	4,000	800	5	$ 1,800
Metering rod N	7,000	700	10	3,500
Vacuum unit	4,000	1,000	4	14,000
Idle compensator R	800	0	—	1,600
Idle compensator Q	1,000	100	10	2,000
Monojet Body S	20,000	10,000	2	40,000
Monojet Body T	5,000	100	50	10,000
Link rod	3,200	400	8	400
Idle arm	1,800	600	3	700
Jet U	2,400	200	12	480
Jet V	14,000	2,000	7	2,800
Idle screw	50,000	5,000	10	3,400
Housing	7,200	600	12	6,000
Bracket	20,000	500	4	5,000
Bushing	4,800	800	6	800
Spacer	1,600	100	16	1,400
1" screw	72,000	3,000	24	720

Action List: Parts in inventory representing more than $1,000 in value and with inventory supply greater than 6 months.

Part	Stock on Hand (Months)	Value	Action
Metering rod N	10	$ 3,500	none
Idle compensator R	(obsolete)	1,600	scrap
Idle compensator Q	10	2,000	rework
Monojet Body T	50	10,000	rework
Idle screw	10	3,400	none
Housing	12	6,000	return to vendor
Spacer	16	1,400	scrap

Exhibit 12.
How to identify and eliminate slow-moving and obsolete inventory

pany has 90 days of superfluous inventory on hand. The cost of carrying this excess inventory having a value of approximately $30,000 at a 30 percent rate is $9,000.

GENERATING CASH FROM EXCESS INVENTORY

Since excess, damaged or obsolete inventory represents not only an ongoing cost but also a potential source of cash, an efficient program to dispose of these inventories is essential for maintaining a healthy cash flow. Some of the key elements of such a program are:

Identify. Your inventory record-keeping system should not be just an accounting device. It should serve as a tool for identifying and isolating unwanted inventories. And it should tell you why the inventory is excess: the product is obsolete, the items are damaged, an ordering error was made, etc. This date will help you to hold inventory excess to a minimum in the future.

Naturally, you will have to look beyond inventory records in your analysis. What are the sales levels of the item or the related product? How long since the last sale? What is company policy on servicing the related product? Decisions about excess inventory can be difficult. Try to devise as many concrete criteria as possible to aid your judgment of what stocks should no longer be retained.

Write off. Your accounting treatment of excess inventory will depend on your industry and tax regulations. Be sure that your company has a definite strategy about write-offs and sticks to it. Your treatment should track as closely as possible with your actual disposal of inventory. Usually, the write-off reserve will be a percentage of sales for the period.

Dispose. Once you've decided to rid yourself of excess inventory, don't backtrack. Storage costs continue even on items that have been written off. Decide on the best strategy for generating cash from the items and act immediately.

Reduced price sales may be the easiest way to move some items, especially at retail. If you choose this route, set specific deadlines for subsequent further reductions and final disposal.

The return-to-vendor option may be viable for some stocks. Consider the discount plus shipping and handling costs.

Scrap is the most common way of disposing of excess inventory in manufacturing. Be realistic in your approach to scrap. Don't let inventory or production managers hoard stocks by citing the cost of reacquiring or remaking the parts. Once the decision has been made to scrap, carry it out in the most efficient way. Smaller lots can often be combined in bins of like materials to be sold. You may want to try bid sales for scrapped stocks that could prove useful for other companies.

Review. Don't let your disposal program be haphazard. Regularly review inventory levels. Compare excess inventory from one period to the next. Keep track of how much was realized through various methods of disposal for each type of inventory. Use the data in your decisions about the feasibility of disposal in the future.

CASH FLOW ALERT

Look for opportunities to enhance cash flow as you dispose of excess inventory. For example, one discount retail chain found that it had an overstock of ice chests in late summer. In order to dispose of the items quickly, the retailer used them in a promotion, giving them away to customers who purchased at least $20 worth of goods. The promotion drew enough additional business to cover the cost of the ice chests. What use can you find for your excess inventories? Would donating them to charity result in a tax benefit that would outweigh the cash they might draw as scrap? Be creative.

MATERIALS REQUIREMENT PLANNING

Materials requirement planning (MRP) is a system which uses computers to tie together production needs and inventory levels. Essentially, it is a scheduling system. Production plans, along with a detailed list of all materials and components, are entered into the computer. These are compared against the availability of items needed and the lead times necessary to make or acquire anything not on hand.

MRP provides many benefits to the company for which it is suited. These include shortened lead times, better use of production resources, improved customer service, and better forecasting and planning.

One of its fundamental paybacks is in reduced inventory. A smaller supply of raw materials inventory can support the same level of production because planning is more detailed and accurate.

For example, the Smith Water Pump Corporation using MRP decides to produce a certain quantity of a particular pump beginning two months from now. The computer program looks at all the components of the pump and compares them to current inventory records. It recognizes that a particular valve will be needed for the assembly, and that not enough of these values are in stock. The computer notes that the lead time between order and delivery of the valve is two weeks. Therefore, it indicates the time when the order should be placed and the quantity that should be ordered. The part is delivered when it is needed. The valve inventory is held at a minimum, yet production proceeds smoothly.

One of the reasons that MRP has become popular is the growing recognition of the cash flow effects of improved inventory management. But an MRP program can be expensive to install and operate. However, the resulting cash flow improvements normally justify the cost.

Exhibit 13 gives a hypothetical case of improved cash flow potential from an MRP project for a company in the $10 million sales range. The firm operates the system on a rented computer costing $4,000 per month. This example was devised by MRP consultant R. Michael Donovan. It is adapted from his book *Manufacturing Resource Planning: Is It Worth It?*

In this example, there is a positive net cash flow of $2,826,500 over the five-year-period. Carrying cost savings far exceed computer and software costs. About 50 percent of the cash flow generation comes from lower inventories—that is, cash that does not have to be invested in inventory.

MRP, in this typical case, improves average inventory turnover by 50 percent. A company with an inventory of $16 million can save $1 million or more a year in carrying costs at current interest rates.

If you are interested in knowing more about MRP, you can write to:

> The American Production and Inventory Control Society
> Watergate Office Building Suite 504
> 2600 Virginia Avenue N.W.
> Washington, D.C. 20037

CASH FLOW ALERT

Parts numbers can serve as more than just a housekeeping tool. A companywide system of part numbers will improve the efficiency of inventory management as well as help uncover opportunities for standardization or substitution. Be alert, too, for identical parts or materials purchased under different vendor names. Such purchases can be combined for bulk discounts and more efficient inventory handling.

ACCOUNTING FOR INVENTORIES

Your accounting treatment of inventory may also have a major impact on your firm's cash flow, particularly in highly inflationary times. The two basic methods of valuing inventory are:

FOX MANUFACTURING CORPORATION
PROJECTED AFTER-TAX CASH FLOW ($000's)
MRP PROJECT

Estimated Savings	Year 1	Year 2	Year 3	Year 4	Year 5
Inventory carrying costs	$ 75.0	$150.0	$225.0	$225.0	$225.0
Obsolescence reduction	30.0	60.0	60.0	60.0	60.0
Labor productivity	81.0	202.5	202.5	202.5	202.5
Direct material	40.0	150.0	150.0	150.0	150.0
Supervisory effectiveness	28.0	70.0	70.0	70.0	70.0
SAVINGS	254.0	632.5	707.5	707.5	707.5
Estimated Costs					
Computer hardware	48.0	48.0	48.0	48.0	48.0

Exhibit 13.
Cash flow analysis of materials requirements planning (MRP)

HOW TO HANDLE OBSOLETE AND EXCESS INVENTORY AND GUARD AGAINST THEFT 49

Software	70.0			
Consulting and education	50.0	30.0		
System support	30.0	20.0		
COSTS	198.0	98.0	48.0	48.0
SAVINGS MINUS COSTS	56.0	534.5	659.5	659.5
INCOME TAX @ 50%	28.0	267.3	329.8	329.8
After-tax profit	28.0	267.2	329.7	329.7
Cash generation from inventory	500.0	500.0		
Investment tax credit on software	7.0			
Depreciation impact on taxes @ 50%	5.3	7.7	7.4	7.4
Net Cash Flow *(after-tax)*	540.3	774.95	837.15	337.1
Cumulative Cash Flow	$540.3	$1,315.2	$2,152.3	$2,489.4	$2,826.5

Exhibit 13. *(Continued)*

- First in, first out (FIFO). This system most accurately reflects the actual situation and the "real" or replacement value of inventory. The inventory value is based on the price of recently purchased items, not on the prices prevailing when the inventory was originally accumulated.
- Last in, first out (LIFO). If you purchased 5,000 units of a particular item last year at $1 per unit, LIFO values your inventory at $5,000 even though you have maintained the inventory by purchasing items this year at $1.50 per unit.

In inflationary times, LIFO accounting improves cash flow. The reason? LIFO assumes that the inventory units going into production are the more expensive, recently purchased ones. As a result, the cost of goods sold will be higher than under FIFO even though no additional cash expenses are incurred. The higher cost of goods sold means lower reported profit, and thus lower taxes. Thus, the total cash flow is improved. This assumes that taxing authorities recognize LIFO accounting.

For example, using the figures mentioned above, assume a company is selling each unit for $2. Taxes are charged at a rate of 50 percent. The effect on cash flow is illustrated by the following table:

	FIFO Accounting	LIFO Accounting
Revenue	$ 10,000	$ 10,000
Reported cost of goods sold	(5,000)	(7,500)
Reported profit	5,000	2,500
Tax @ 50%	(2,500)	(1,250)
Profit	2,500	1,250
Less increase in inventory	2,500	—
Net cash flow	$ —	$ 1,250

While the profit under LIFO is lower, the tax payment is lower, which represents an improvement in cash flow of $1,250. The amount spent for new inventory in the year is the same $7,500 in each case.

INVENTORY AND SECURITY

If you don't recognize the significant impact of security losses on cash flow, start by considering some of the common fallacies in thinking about the subject:

"It can't happen here." Employee theft alone accounts for more than $50 billion in losses for U.S. businesses every year. Retailers lose an estimated 1.1 percent of total revenues to employee and customer dishonesty. And security experts agree that those companies which take the attitude that they're immune from the problem are the most likely candidates for losses.

"It's a cost of doing business." No. Security losses are a direct drain on cash flow, and they are not inevitable.

"We leave it to the professionals." You hire your own security force or contract guards. Security is their job, you think. Wrong. Every level of management and all employees should be actively involved in the prevention of security losses. A security guard is your last line of defense against theft. Alert, security-conscious employees are your first and most effective line.

HOW SECURITY LOSSES HURT CASH FLOW

Excess inventory harms cash flow because of the extra capital tied up in the goods, as well as the other carrying costs. The loss of inventory through theft, however, has a much more damaging impact on cash flow.

Consider, for example, the company which manufactures power hand tools. The driver of one of the firm's trucks takes home a drill that sells for $100. The company makes a gross profit margin of 10 percent. Potential cash flow has been reduced by $100. In order to make up for this single loss, the firm will have to sell an additional $1,000 worth of goods.

A consideration of the severe impact of security losses on cash flow should jolt both managers and employees out of the complacent attitude that such thefts are "part of doing business." You should particularly emphasize this fact to employees who are likely to look on the theft of company property as a fringe benefit.

CASH FLOW ALERT

The best way to tune the security department into the cash flow effort is to turn it into a profit center. Companies which see the security function as only a cost are likely to feel they're saving cash by scrimping on security efforts. But the firm that realizes that $1 spent on security cuts profit-draining losses by $10 will view security spending as a way of improving cash flow. Accurate records or past security losses, plus documented improvement resulting from new security measures, combine to present the department in this light. Emphasize payback on security expenditures, not cost.

LIMITING THE CASH FLOW IMPACT OF SECURITY LOSSES

Every business must take steps to recognize potential loss areas and to introduce cost-effective ways of limiting losses. The idea should always be to prevent the loss, not to try to catch criminals after the fact. Here are a few hints for improving your cash flow by protecting inventories:

Build in security. Design warehouse and production facilities with security in mind. Safe storage areas away from exits pay off.

Use lighting. Adequate lighting, particularly around valuable inventory and stocks stored outside, is one of the cheapest and most effective ways to protect yourself against losses.

Limit mobility. Keep visitors away from vulnerable inventory. Store high-value items in a separate area and require employees to have a special pass to gain access.

Control the stock room. An attended stock room should have a double door so that the stock clerk can pass out supplies without having other employees actually enter the room.

Isolate shipping, receiving, and storage areas. Never combine receiving and shipping docks. Move inventory quickly off platforms into storage. Limit access of drivers to storage areas.

Recognize risks. Prime targets for theft are inventory items which are high in value, easy to resell, and simple to transport. For example, a manufacturer of computer chips lost $20 million in one weekend. Thieves took away the company's entire stock of semiconductors in a pickup truck. Scarcity made the items easy to resell.

Policy. A clear policy on employee theft costs nothing and can save a great deal in losses. What is and is not considered proper behavior? Spell it out, give the document to every worker, and require each one to read and sign it.

Unannounced inspections. They may ruffle employee feathers, but they're an effective way to cut down on pilfering.

Controls. Have workers sign for tools. Make sure paperwork is not being completed haphazardly. Number all forms and account for them. Check on the reasons for voided forms. Separate responsibilities where security temptations are apparent.

Consciousness. Maintain the readiness of your employees in the war against theft. Posters, awards, leaflets and supervisors' encouragement can all help make employees security conscious. Be sure employees understand the true impact of "minor" theft.

CASH FLOW ALERT

A "security environment" can help cut losses while minimizing expenses. For example, some firms supplement a closed-circuit television surveillance system with bogus cameras. The fake devices look like the real ones and deter theft in the same way for a fraction of the cost. Book retailers set up detectors at their doors which react to magnetic strips built into the books. But while all books are "demagnetized" at the cash register, costs are held down by including the strip in only a small percent of the books. Public awareness of the security device deters theft in itself.

5

GETTING THE MOST CASH FLOW OUT OF PURCHASE VOLUME DISCOUNTS

Inventory represents a major area of working-capital investment which can easily and uneconomically tie up large amounts of cash. Purchases of raw materials often provide many opportunities for cash flow improvement because of their timing, size, and the seller's pricing terms. A careful cash flow analysis of the effects of purchase volume discounts, for example, is necessary to determine their real value. Keep in mind that purchase volume discounts affect not only the total amount of your company's cash flow, but its timing as well.

THE KRAKEN CONTAINER CORPORATION

The purchasing manager of the Kraken Container Corporation is routinely taking all discounts that vendors offer for volume purchases. His reason is simple: the lower the price he pays for each material or component, the lower the total cost of the finished product and thus the higher the profit. He thinks his reasoning is sound, but he is overlooking his firm's cost of money and cash flow requirements.

What he does not consider carefully is the cash flow implications of his actions. Exhibit 14 lists the four materials that go into his com-

55

Material	Price	Annual Use (Units)	Total Use Value	Discount Terms on Volume Purchase	Inventory Carrying Cost	Months of Inventory in Discount Amount
Benzene	$1.50/gallon	100,000	$150,000	6% on 25,000 gallons	30%	3.0
Polypropylene	$ .38/pound	500,000	190,000	2% on 200,000 pounds	20%	4.8
Stainless wire	$4.00/pound	30,000	120,000	5% on 10,000 pounds	40%	4.0
Sheet steel	$ .30/pound	600,000	180,000	8% on 500,000 pounds	20%	10.0

Exhibit 14.
Raw materials purchase discounts and carrying cost analysis

pany's major products. The discount offered by vendors for volume purchases range from 2 percent to 9 percent of the regular price. The purchasing manager assumes that each of the discounts contributes to the product's profit margin.

THE BREAK-EVEN DISCOUNT

Volume discounts are designed to have you purchase larger quantities and maintain a higher level of inventory than you normally require. In the case of Kraken, for example, the purchasing manager has to buy a three-months' supply of benzene and a ten-months' supply of sheet steel to receive the discounts offered by the vendors. Supply, order, and carrying cost considerations, discussed in Chapter 3, suggest that Kraken purchase only a single month's worth of each of the materials at a time. The extra inventory purchase to obtain the volume discounts, therefore, ranges from two to nine months.

The purchasing manager can do a break-even analysis of the bulk purchase discounts to evaluate the cash flow effects of his buying tactics. The discount percent that is needed to balance the increased cost of carrying the extra inventory is equal to the average excess inventory in months divided by 12 multiplied by the carrying cost expressed in decimal form. The *average* excess inventory is one-half of the excess amount purchased.

For example, take the case of benzene in Exhibit 14. The company uses 100,000 gallons of the solvent each year. To obtain the 6 percent volume discount, the firm must purchase 25,000 gallons at one time. This is equal to three months of inventory, which is two months over the one-month purchase amount at the regular price.

To find the break-even discount for benzene, the purchasing manager applies the formula:

$$\frac{BE}{Discount} = \frac{\text{Excess months of material purchased}/2}{12} \times \text{inventory carrying cost}$$

$$\frac{2/2}{12} \times .30 = .025 = 2.5\%$$

The formula shows that a discount of 2.5 percent will cover Kraken's cost of carrying the extra inventory. Since the vendor is offering a 6 percent discount for volume purchases of benzene, Kraken's purchasing manager is justified in taking the discount and buying this material in bulk.

Note that the break-even formula is based on the carrying cost of the inventory. It assumes that ordering costs are fixed and will not be affected by spot decisions regarding discounts and volume quantities. The carrying cost will also be affected by the amount of the discount. The formula, therefore, produces a slightly higher discount than is actually required to break even.

Next the purchasing manager examines the discount offer on polypropylene. Here the company uses 500,000 pounds of the material in a year. To obtain the 2 percent discount, a purchase of at least 200,000 pounds has to be made. This represents a 4.8-months' supply of the material, or 3.8 months in excess of the normal purchase quantity.

Using the formula again, the manager finds the break-even discount:

$$\frac{3.8/2}{12} \times .20 = .032 = 3.2\%$$

Kraken is receiving only a 2 percent discount on the purchase. That means a reduced cash flow from carrying the excess inventory. The firm, in effect, is paying more for the material than if it purchased it at the higher price on a monthly basis in lower volumes. Taking the 2 percent volume discount is unwise.

A quick way to evaluate purchased materials and components in terms of volume discounts and the related cash flow implications is to use the chart in Exhibit 15. To improve the cash flow, a volume discount for the purchase of a certain amount of excess inventory must fall *above* the line which represents the inventory's carrying cost rate. The discounts offered, as well as the break-even discounts for Kraken's four purchased materials, are indicated on the chart.

Benzene, product A, is plotted on the 30 percent carrying cost line. The break-even discount rate is positioned on this line at the two-months' excess inventory point using the horizontal scale. The actual

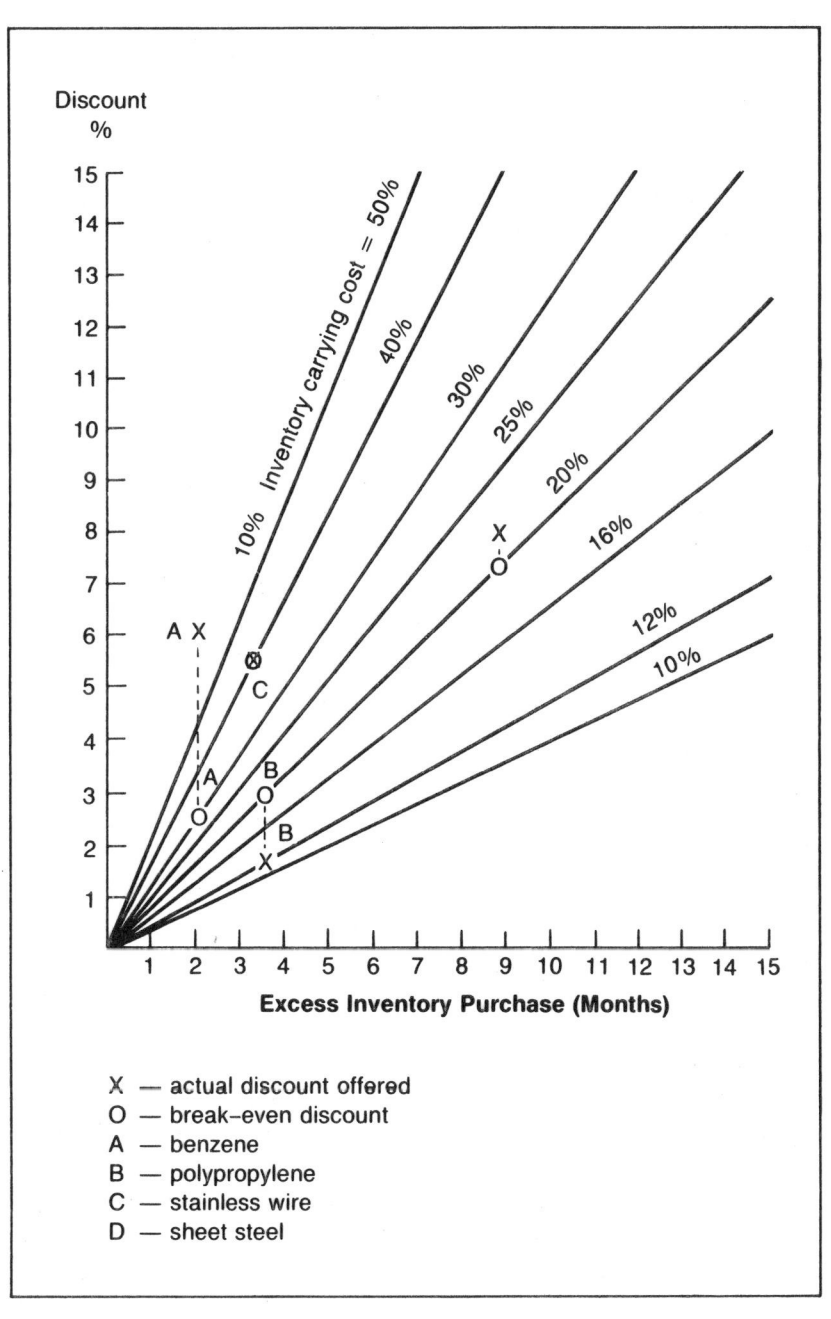

Exhibit 15.
Break-even analysis of volume discounts

discount of 6 percent is then plotted using the vertical discount percent scale. Since the actual discount point is above the 30 percent carrying cost line, it exceeds the break-even discount rate.

The chart shows that the 2 percent discount offered by the polypropylene, product B, vendor is below Kraken's break-even rate for this product. The stainless wire, product C, bulk discount and break-even rate are the same. Sheet steel, product D, has a discount slightly higher than the break-even rate.

CASH FLOW ALERT

You can use this chart and your own company's carrying costs for major purchased materials to quickly determine whether an offer of a special volume discount will improve or worsen your cash flow.

THE QUESTION OF TIMING

The timing of the cash inflows and outlays is also important to consider when evaluating cash discounts. Sometimes a discount will involve the purchase of a year's supply or more of inventory. A generous discount may indicate that the offer is worthwhile because the discount more than offsets the cost of carrying the inventory.

But the purchasing manager must give the situation additional thought before acting. Perhaps the company will have to take no more bank debt at a higher rate in order to pay out the cash in advance. This may raise the cost of carrying the inventory. If so, it will require recalculation of the cash flow value of the discount.

Perhaps, too, the necessary financing is not currently available. This could mean a future cash shortage. Tying up cash in inventories, despite a substantial discount, may disrupt operations and preclude other investments that are highly profitable.

The purchasing manager at Kraken took this factor into account in evaluating the next two materials, stainless wire and sheet steel.

The break-even discount rate on the stainless wire is the same 5 percent that the vendor is offering. Since the material is in abundant supply and the price has been stable in recent months, there is no incentive to spend cash for excess inventory.

Buying the wire on a monthly basis also leaves open the possibility of switching vendors for a better price. And, if the company's demand for the wire increases, speeding inventory turns, then the manager can decide to take advantage of the volume discount. In the current situation, however, both his flexibility and cash position are improved by not taking the volume discount.

The situation with sheet steel is slightly more complex. The manager's break-even analysis (Exhibit 15) indicates that the discount is worth taking. The price differential, though, only barely offsets the carrying cost. In addition, the purchase of steel in bulk to obtain the 8 percent discount requires a cash outlay of $138,000.

The manager realizes that timing is important. Kraken is a small company with limited financial resources, and it is particularly sensitive to cash flow imbalances, even if they are temporary. To judge the effect of the volume discounts on the timing of the cash flows, the manager has to look at the total cash flow impact.

IMPACT ON CASH FLOW

To get a complete picture of the overall effect of volume discounts on Kraken's cash flow, the purchasing manager sets up several pro forma cash budgets for this particular product line. The budgets show estimates of the month-by-month sales for the year. The four purchased materials under consideration account for about 50 percent of the product's price. Labor costs associated with the product account for another 40 percent. He obtains the information he needs from the accounting department. The pro forma cash flow budgets also break out the costs of the materials and the carrying cost of the inventory.

The budget in Exhibit 16 shows the cash flow effect of taking all of the volume discounts on the purchase of the materials. The budget in Exhibit 17 shows the cash flow situation if only the discounts indicated by the break-even analysis are taken.

MANAGING CASH FLOW

	January	February	March	April	May	June
Sales	$120,000	$120,000	$120,000	$100,000	$100,000	$130,000
Labor costs	48,000	48,000	48,000	40,000	40,000	52,000
Materials Costs						
Benzene	—	36,000	—	—	36,000	—
Polypropylene	74,480	—	—	—	74,480	—
Stainless wire	—	—	38,000	—	—	—
Sheet steel	—	—	—	138,000	—	—
Inventory Carrying Costs (averaged)						
Benzene	450	450	450	450	450	450
Polypropylene	621	621	621	621	621	621
Stainless wire	633	633	633	633	633	633
Sheet steel	1,150	1,150	1,150	1,150	1,150	1,150
CASH FLOW	$(5,334)	$33,146	$(80,854)	$(53,334)	$75,146	$43,146

Exhibit 16.
Monthly cash flows with taking all volume discounts

GETTING THE MOST CASH FLOW OUT OF PURCHASE VOLUME DISCOUNTS 63

	July	August	September	October	November	December
Sales	$140,000	$140,000	$140,000	$140,000	$120,000	$120,000
Labor costs	56,000	56,000	56,000	56,000	48,000	48,000
Materials Costs						
Benzene	—	36,000	—	—	36,000	—
Polypropylene	—	—	—	74,480	—	—
Stainless wire	38,000	—	—	—	38,000	—
Sheet steel	—	—	—	—	—	—
Inventory Carrying Costs (averaged)						
Benzene	450	450	450	450	450	450
Polypropylene	621	621	621	621	621	621
Stainless wire	633	633	633	633	633	633
Sheet steel	1,150	1,150	1,150	1,150	1,150	1,150
CASH FLOW	$ 43,146	$ 45,146	$ 81,146	$ 6,666	$(4,854)	$ 69,146

Exhibit 16. *(Continued)*

MANAGING CASH FLOW

	January	February	March	April	May	June
Sales	$120,000	$120,000	$120,000	$100,000	$100,000	$130,000
Labor costs	48,000	48,000	48,000	40,000	40,000	52,000
Materials Costs						
Benzene	—	36,000	—	—	36,000	—
Polypropylene	15,833	15,833	15,833	15,833	15,833	15,833
Stainless wire	10,000	10,000	10,000	10,000	10,000	10,000
Sheet steel	—	—	—	138,000	—	—
Inventory Carrying Costs (averaged)						
Benzene	450	450	450	450	450	450
Polypropylene	132	132	132	132	132	132
Stainless wire	167	167	167	167	167	167
Sheet steel	1,150	1,150	1,150	1,150	1,150	1,150
CASH FLOW	$ 44,268	$ 8,268	$(105,732)	$ 3,732	$ 50,268	$ 56,268

Exhibit 17.
Monthly cash flows excluding some volume discounts

GETTING THE MOST CASH FLOW OUT OF PURCHASE VOLUME DISCOUNTS

	July	August	September	October	November	December
Sales	$140,000	$140,000	$140,000	$140,000	$120,000	$120,000
Labor costs	56,000	56,000	56,000	56,000	48,000	48,000
Materials Costs						
Benzene	—	36,000	—	—	36,000	—
Polypropylene	15,833	15,833	15,833	15,833	15,833	15,833
Stainless wire	10,000	10,000	10,000	10,000	10,000	10,000
Sheet steel	—	—	—	—	—	—
Inventory Carrying Costs (averaged)						
Benzene	450	450	450	450	450	450
Polypropylene	132	132	132	132	132	132
Stainless wire	167	167	167	167	167	167
Sheet steel	1,150	1,150	1,150	1,150	1,150	1,150
CASH FLOW	$ 56,268	$ 20,268	$ 56,268	$ 56,268	$ 8,268	$ 44,268

Exhibit 17. *(Continued)*

Comparing the monthly cash flows illustrates that the company pays slightly more for the materials by not taking all the discounts but that the overall cash flow is improved by $1,665, as seen below:

	All Discounts Taken	Some Discounts Not Taken
Sales	$1,490,000	$1,490,000
Labor costs	596,000	596,000
Materials Costs		
Benzene	$141,000	$141,000
Polypropylene	186,200	190,000
Stainless wire	114,000	120,000
Sheet steel	165,600	165,600
Total	606,800	616,600
Inventory Carrying Costs		
Benzene	5,400	5,400
Polypropylene	7,448	1,583
Stainless wire	7,600	2,000
Sheet steel	13,800	13,800
Total	34,248	22,783
CASH FLOW	$ 252,952	$ 254,617

He also notes in Exhibit 17 that the monthly cash flows are less erratic. Volume discounts tend to make cash flow more erratic because they require substantial outlays of cash at one time. See Exhibits 16 and 17.

This brings the manager back to a decision on sheet steel. It is apparent from both the cash budgets that the purchase of the steel in bulk necessitates a considerable outlay of cash in April. While there

GETTING THE MOST CASH FLOW OUT OF PURCHASE VOLUME DISCOUNTS

may be nothing basically wrong with occasional monthly negative cash flows, he must look at the situation in the light of his own company's financial position.

The purchasing manager, therefore, prepares a third cash budget which evaluates the monthly cash flows if the sheet steel is not purchased in bulk. While the total cash flow is $2,100 less than it would be if the steel were purchased at a discount, as seen below, Exhibit 18 shows that the swings in the monthly cash flows have been reduced further and that there is no negative cash flow in April.

Sales		$1,490,000
Labor Costs		596,000
Materials Costs		
Benzene	$141,000	
Polypropylene	190,000	
Stainless wire	120,000	
Sheet steel	180,000	
Total		631,000
Inventory Carrying Costs (averaged)		
Benzene	$ 5,400	
Polypropylene	1,583	
Stainless wire	2,000	
Sheet steel	1,500	
Total		10,483
CASH FLOW		$252,517

The purchasing manager then discusses the analysis with Kraken's treasurer. There is a projected shortage of cash resources during April and May, and together they decide that it would be better to forgo the discount and buy the steel on a monthly basis.

MANAGING CASH FLOW

	January	February	March	April	May	June
Sales	$120,000	$120,000	$120,000	$100,000	$100,000	$130,000
Labor costs	48,000	48,000	48,000	40,000	40,000	52,000
Materials Costs						
Benzene	—	36,000	—	—	36,000	—
Polypropylene	15,833	15,833	15,833	15,833	15,833	15,833
Stainless wire	10,000	10,000	10,000	10,000	10,000	10,000
Sheet steel	15,000	15,000	15,000	15,000	15,000	15,000
Inventory Carrying Costs (averaged)						
Benzene	450	450	450	450	450	450
Polypropylene	132	132	132	132	132	132
Stainless wire	167	167	167	167	167	167
Sheet steel	125	125	125	125	125	125
CASH FLOW	$ 30,293	$(5,707)	$ 30,293	$ 18,293	$(17,707)	$ 36,293

Exhibit 18.
Monthly cash flows excluding sheet steel discount

GETTING THE MOST CASH FLOW OUT OF PURCHASE VOLUME DISCOUNTS

	July	August	September	October	November	December
Sales	$140,000	$140,000	$140,000	$140,000	$120,000	$120,000
Labor costs	56,000	56,000	56,000	56,000	48,000	48,000
Materials Costs						
Benzene	—	36,000	—	—	36,000	—
Polypropylene	15,833	15,833	15,833	15,833	15,833	15,833
Stainless wire	10,000	10,000	10,000	10,000	10,000	10,000
Sheet steel	15,000	15,000	15,000	15,000	15,000	15,000
Inventory Carrying Costs (averaged)						
Benzene	450	450	450	450	450	450
Polypropylene	132	132	132	132	132	132
Stainless wire	167	167	167	167	167	167
Sheet steel	125	125	125	125	125	125
CASH FLOW	$ 42,293	$ 6,293	$ 42,293	$ 42,293	$(5,707)	$ 30,293

Exhibit 18. *(Continued)*

CASH FLOW ALERT

The break-even analysis for volume discounts is also an excellent tool to use in price negotiations with vendors. For example, you can use it to point out that the vendor's across-the-board volume discount schedule is not economical for your firm from a cash flow point of view. You can also demonstrate convincingly how a slightly higher discount, or a reduction in the volume needed to qualify for the discount, could help your company to overcome the barriers to buying in bulk.

6

CONTROLLING ACCOUNTS RECEIVABLE

Too often managers relegate the credit control function and responsibility to subordinates. This can be a very costly mistake since credit is one of the most fundamental aspects of managing a business. Lack of a sound credit policy and effective control can lead quickly to "runaway" collection periods and costs plus bad debts and severe cash flow problems.

Trade receivables represent an important factor in the cash flow picture because:

- The greater the amount of funds tied up in accounts receivable, the greater the overall delay in cash inflows
- Lengthier accounts outstanding mean increased risk to future cash flow
- Larger accounts receivable amounts mean a larger investment in working capital for each dollar of sales.

There would be no cash flow problems if it were possible to eliminate trade receivables by selling only for cash. Competitive pressures, long-standing customs, and facilitation of trade, all virtually require most firms to offer sales on credit.

Payment terms can vary by type of industry and by country. They may range from cash on delivery to cash within 7 days to payment 60, 90, or even more days in the future. Your goal from a cash flow perspective is to hold receivables to the minimum possible amount in light of the business environment in which you operate.

EFFECT ON CASH FLOW

The effects of various receivables situations on actual cash inflows can be significant, as the following example illustrates.

Socam Distributing Co. supplies retail hardware stores with a variety of do-it-yourself tools. The firm sells to its customers on terms of net 60 days. Enforcement of these terms has been lax, however. Some customers pay more slowly. So while Socam's sales currently average $2 million a month, accounts receivable total $6 million. The company finances the receivables with short-term bank loans for which it pays 22 percent annual interest.

Socam's controller was interested in finding out the effect of the firm's receivables situation on its cash flow. To do so, he evaluated cash flow under current conditions and in three hypothetical situations, each time isolating the cash flow effect of the outstanding accounts as follows:

1. Current terms are strictly enforced.
2. Terms of net 30 days are applied and strictly enforced.
3. All customers are required to pay cash.

Exhibit 19 gives the results of his analysis. The numbers illustrate the considerable effect that accounts receivable strategies have on cash flow. Simply by enforcing its current terms and collecting funds within 60 days of sale, for example, Socam could improve net cash flow by $33,000, or 33 percent! More stringent terms might give a further boost to cash flow. If the firm was able to enforce a policy of cash sales without losing customers, net cash flow would double. This assumes that no sales would be lost which might not be realistic.

CONTROLLING ACCOUNTS RECEIVABLE

($000)	Current Situation	Situation No. 1 (60 Days Credit)	Situation No. 2 (30 Days Credit)	Situation No. 3 (No Credit)
Sales	$2,000	$2,000	$2,000	$2,000
Cost of sales @ 90% of selling price	1,800	1,800	1,800	1,800
Gross cash flow	200	200	200	200
Accounts receivable outstanding	$6,000	$4,000	$2,000	0
Cost of A/R (90%)	5,400	3,600	1,800	0
Monthly cost to carry accounts receivable @ 22%	99	66	33	0
Net cash flow	$ 101	$ 134	$ 167	$ 200

Exhibit 19.
Cash flow effect of credit policy

DAYS SALES OUTSTANDING

The total amount of accounts receivable outstanding varies according to two factors. The first is the amount of sales during recent periods. The second is the rate at which accounts are collected. Studying gross receivable amounts will not reveal which factor is accounting for increases or decreases.

The Days Sales Outstanding (DSO) formula isolates the first factor so that attention can be focused on how effective collection efforts are. While it has its limitations, a DSO analysis is the starting point for any program to monitor receivables with the object of improving cash flow. Later you will see how this ratio can be further refined.

Days sales outstanding is the ratio of receivables to sales. You can calculate it easily by dividing your firm's accounts receivable outstanding by average daily sales.

$$DSO = \frac{\text{Accounts receivable outstanding}}{\text{Annual sales}/360}$$

Average daily sales can also be found by dividing sales during the latest quarter or month by the appropriate number of days. While this may give a more accurate picture of DSO in some cases, it can also distort the ratio, especially for companies with seasonal variations in sales levels.

Take, for instance, a company which had sales last year of $3,750,000. At year end, accounts receivables still outstanding totaled $730,000. Days sales outstanding amounted to:

$$\frac{\$730,000}{\$3,750,000/360} = \frac{\$730,000}{\$10,416} = 70.1 \text{ DSO}$$

The DSO ratio is good for looking at the gross effects of receivables on cash flow. For example, Exhibit 20 indicates the total effect on cash flow for each $1 million in annual sales for various carrying costs and DSO levels.

Exhibit 20 and the examples in this chapter calculate the cost effect of accounts receivable on the basis of the cost of sales, rather than on the face amount of the accounts outstanding. From a cost perspective, this gives a clearer picture of the consequences, since this

% Carrying Cost of Receivables	Days Sales Outstanding					
	15	30	45	60	90	120
5	$ 1,667	$ 3,333	$ 5,000	$ 6,667	$10,000	$13,333
10	3,333	6,667	10,000	13,333	20,000	26,667
12	4,000	8,000	12,000	16,000	24,000	32,000
15	5,000	10,000	15,000	20,000	30,000	40,000
18	6,000	12,000	18,000	24,000	36,000	48,000
20	6,667	13,333	20,000	26,667	40,000	53,333
22	7,333	14,667	22,000	29,333	44,000	58,667
25	8,333	16,667	25,000	33,333	50,000	66,667
30	10,000	20,000	30,000	40,000	60,000	80,000
32	10,667	21,333	32,000	42,667	64,000	85,333
35	11,667	23,333	35,000	46,667	70,000	93,333

Note: The cash flow effect is based on the cost of sales, which is 80 percent of sales.

Exhibit 20.
Cash flow effect from $1 million in sales

represents the actual amount of cash the company has invested in its receivables.

For example, a company has to borrow funds at a rate of 18 percent to finance receivables. Its sales are $5 million a year. The DSO is 45. The receivables cost $500,000, which has a negative impact on cash flow of $90,000 ($500,000 × 0.18) due to the carrying charge. If the company can improve its collection of accounts so that its DSO is brought down to 30 (accounts receivable of $416,667), then the carrying cost will drop to $75,000 for a $37,500 increase in annual cash flow as a result of stepping up collections. There will also be a onetime cash flow increase of $208,333 from reducing the amount of outstanding receivables.

Another point to note from Exhibit 20 is the cost of adding sales. For example, if a company's DSO is 60 and its carrying cost is 25 percent, then a $2 million annual sales increase will affect cash flow by:

> Requiring an immediate $333,333 investment in receivables (60 days cost of sales)
> Draining $66,666 of cash flow each year as a result of the carrying costs of 25 percent.

These amounts must be taken into account when projecting the total cash flow from added sales. For instance, if the marginal profit on the sales is $400,000 (20 percent), the net cash flow in the first year is zero.

AGING RECEIVABLES

Total days sales outstanding do not tell the whole story about a company's receivables. Consider two firms with identical DSO ratios. Monthly sales are $10,000. Each company has $30,000 in receivables outstanding. But the makeup of these amounts is as follows:

Length of Time Outstanding	Company A Amount	Company A Percent of Total Receivables	Company B Amount	Company B Percent of Total Receivables
Current	$10,000	33%	$10,000	33%
30 days	15,000	50	6,000	20
60 days	4,000	13	5,000	17
90 days	1,000	3	5,000	17
120 days+	0	—	4,000	13
Total	$30,000	100%	$30,000	100%

While the DSO level is 90 for each company, the receivables situation and risk for each company is different. At Company A, 83 percent of receivables is paid within 60 days of the invoice. At Company B, however, only 53 percent of the accounts is collected within this period.

The major effect on cash flow for Company B comes in the form of the increased risk of bad debts. If, for example, bad debt experience averages 5 percent of accounts in the 90–120 days category and 20 percent of accounts over 120 days due, then Company A can expect only $50 in bad debts from its current receivables. Company B, though, faces potential bad debts of $1,050. The effect of this bad debt risk on cash flow can be enormous.

Exhibit 21 gives an example of an aging report compiled by one company covering the preceding six months. The firm sells on terms of net 60 days but offers a 1 percent discount for payment within 30 days. All accounts outstanding after 60 days are overdue.

The first part of the report, shown in Chart A, points to several factors which may affect the company's cash flow. First, there is a growing percentage of receivables in the overdue category. This indicates that customers are, on the whole, taking longer to pay their bills. Stepped-up collection efforts are called for to reduce total receivables, cut the firm's exposure to bad debts, and improve cash flow.

There is also some growth in both the percentage and amount of accounts due more than 120 days. These receivables are particularly difficult to collect. They will soon have to be written off as bad debts. The trend should not be allowed to continue. The company should analyze these accounts in order to find out how more-stringent credit standards can reverse the situation. Perhaps more thorough investigation of customers' financial standings is called for, which is covered in Chapter 8.

Chart B in Exhibit 21 approaches the aging of receivables differently. Rather than look at all receivables each month, it tracks the collection schedule of each month's sales. First it lists the amount of sales paid within 30 days along with the percent of original sales. Next it lists the amount and percent of sales paid within 60 days, and so on.

This approach compensates for variations in monthly sales. For example, in Chart A, 30-day receivables in April make up a large portion of that month's total compared with other periods. But Chart B shows that that increase is the result of high March sales. March customers have actually paid more quickly than others—54 percent

($000)
Chart A

Receivables Outstanding

Month		Current	30-Day	60-Day	90-Day	120-Day+	Percent Overdue	Total
January	$	$2,800	$1,200	$400	$80	$20		$4,500
	%	62.2	26.7	8.9	1.8	.4	11.1%	
February	$	3,200	1,400	600	70	30		5,300
	%	60.4	26.4	11.3	1.3	.6	13.2	
March	$	4,800	1,500	680	100	40		7,120
	%	67.4	21.1	9.6	1.4	.6	11.6	
April	$	2,800	2,200	580	120	30		5,730
	%	48.9	38.4	10.1	2.1	.5	12.7	
May	$	2,400	1,500	720	90	50		4,760
	%	50.4	31.5	15.1	1.9	1.1	18.1	
June	$	3,000	1,000	820	160	50		5,030
	%	59.6	19.9	16.3	3.2	1.0	20.5	

Exhibit 21.
Aging report on accounts receivable

CONTROLLING ACCOUNTS RECEIVABLE

Chart B

Receivables Paid

Month		Total Credit Sales	After 30 Days	After 60 Days	After 90 Days	After 120 Days	Receivables Outstanding
January	$	$2,800	$1,400	$2,120	$2,680	$2,750	$ 50
	%		50.0	75.7	95.7	98.2	.8
February	$	3,200	1,700	2,620	3,110	3,150	50
	%		53.1	81.9	97.2	98.4	.6
March	$	4,800	2,600	4,080	4,640	—	160
	%		54.2	85.0	96.6	—	3.3
April	$	2,800	1,300	1,980	—	—	820
	%		46.6	70.7	—	—	29.3
May	$	2,400	1,400	—	—	—	1,000
	%		58.3	—	—	—	41.7

Exhibit 21. *(Continued)*

have paid by the end of April. So, even though $2.2 million remains in 30-day receivables, no real collection problem exists.

But Chart B does point up a problem not immediately apparent in Chart A. Receipts for April sales are coming in more slowly than for previous months. A full 29.3 percent of April sales are becoming overdue at the end of June. This should alert the credit manager to investigate the reasons for the problem. Who are the customers? What product mix was sold in April? What can be done to speed payments?

ANALYZING CUSTOMER ACCOUNTS

Both DSO and aging analyses are very useful when applied to a company's total receivables picture. But to improve cash flow, a firm must also look at receivables in detail. The numbers in Exhibit 22 analyze a flow of Socam Distributing Co.'s individual customers.

Clearly, some customers are much more prompt payers than others. If Socam's average days sales outstanding is 90, B&J and Allied

($000) Customer	Last Year's Sales	Current	30- Day	60- Day	90- Day+	Total	Days Sales Outstanding
B&J Hardware %	$ 50	4 14	6 21	8 29	10 35	28 100	201.6
Allied Building %	$ 200	20 27	30 40	16 21	9 12	75 100	135
Payless Stores %	$ 100	6 33	10 56	2 11	0 —	18 100	64.8
DeWitt Hardware %	$ 150	10 56	8 44	0 —	0 —	18 100	43.2

Exhibit 22.
Aging report on four customers

CONTROLLING ACCOUNTS RECEIVABLE

both pay more slowly than average. Payless and DeWitt are more prompt in settling accounts.

To further analyze these accounts, Socam's credit manager calculated the effect on cash flow of each customer's accounts receivable. The results of this analysis are shown in Exhibit 23.

The figures for B&J Hardware indicate that because of that customer's slow payment practices, Socam is short $544 in net cash flow on annual sales of $50,000. Also, since 35 percent of B&J's receivables have been due for more than 90 days (Exhibit 22), the risk of bad debts is a large one. Any invoice not paid would result in a negative cash flow for the account. Therefore, the current situation with this account is clearly unacceptable. One solution? Begin selling to B&J for cash only until the company has paid all amounts due and restored its credit standing.

With Allied Building, the situation is only slightly better. Net cash flow is $5,150. But Socam has to invest $67,500 to finance Allied's accounts receivables. The resulting cash flow is only 7.6 percent of this investment, not a very substantial rate of return. In addition, Allied has $9,000 in accounts due more than 90 days. Again, Socam should apply much more stringent credit terms to this customer until its DSO is brought down and the return improves.

The situation at Payless Stores and DeWitt Hardware is considerably better. It is worth noting in both cases, though, that even with relatively prompt-paying customers, the cost of carrying accounts receivable does have a substantial impact on cash flow.

CASH FLOW ALERT

If you make credit sales only to your strongest customers, you will have few bad-debt losses. But you will probably lose sales and profits. Always examine the profit on sales in relationship to the costs. Allied Building (Exhibit 23), for example, provides a gross profit of $20,000 versus carrying costs of $14,850. The profit margin is acceptable, but the costs are not. Take action to bring those costs down.

	B&J Hardware	Allied Building	Payless Stores	DeWitt Hardware
Sales	$50,000	$200,000	$100,000	$150,000
Cost of sales (90%)	45,000	180,000	90,000	120,000
Gross cash flow	5,000	20,000	10,000	30,000
Accounts receivable	$28,000	$75,000	$18,000	$18,000
Cost of A/R (90%)	25,200	67,500	16,200	16,200
Carrying cost of A/R @ 22%	5,544	14,850	3,564	3,564
Net cash flow	$ (544)	$ 5,150	$ 6,436	$ 26,436

Exhibit 23.
Cash flow effect of receivables on customers' accounts

7

HOW TO USE A WEIGHTED ANALYSIS TO IMPROVE CASH FLOW

D ays sales outstanding calculations and aging reports do not completely pinpoint the effect of receivables collection patterns on cash flow. The reasons for this are:

- The rate of sales per given period often varies erratically or seasonally. This distorts the calculation of DSO. For example, if sales have declined in a recent period, receivables and average DSO will be down even though collection experience on accounts has not improved.
- Gross aging reports do not take into account the true age of an invoiced amount, the actual number of days from the date of the invoice until the present.

DOLLAR DAYS OUTSTANDING

One way to refine aging and days outstanding calculations is to evaluate receivables using the actual invoice date and to weight each uncollected bill according to its dollar value. An illustration will show that this method allows for a more accurate determination of the impact of receivables on cash flow.

Griffen, Inc. and Dryad Corp. are both in the metal foundry business. Each recorded identical sales in the past year of $24 million. Both companies sell on terms of net 30 days. But slow payments have resulted in receivables of $2,500,000, or 37.5 DSO, for each. The gross aging report below shows that the composition of each company's receivables is identical.

($000)	Current	30-Day	60-Day	90-Day+
Griffen, Inc.	$1,000	$800	$500	$200
Dryad Corp.	1,000	800	500	200

It would be wrong, however, to assume that the cash flow picture at each company is exactly the same in relation to accounts receivable.

Exhibit 24 shows each company's receivables analyzed according to dollar days. First, the gross receivables are broken down by actual invoice amounts. The dollar days represent the invoice amount times the total number of days up to the present since the invoice was issued.

Dollar days outstanding (DDO) are more relevant to cash flow since amounts billed must be financed from the time of the sale, not from the end of the month.

The dollar days analysis indicates several facts which are not illustrated in the gross aging report:

- Griffen has fewer dollar days in current receivables. Since sales are the same at both companies, this *may* indicate that Griffen is lax in sending out invoices at the time of shipment. Late invoicing slows payments and increases receivables.
- Dryad has fewer dollar days for accounts in each category over 30 days. This indicates that collection efforts are more successful than those of Griffen.

(000)	GRIFFEN, INC.		
Receivables Category	Invoice Amount	Days Outstanding	Dollar Days
Current	$ 500	12	6,000
	400	6	2,400
	100	4	400
Total	1,000		8,800
30-day	400	50	20,000
	200	45	9,000
	200	40	8,000
Total	800		37,000
60-day	200	88	17,600
	200	76	15,200
	100	65	6,500
Total	500		39,300
90-day+	100	118	11,800
	100	100	10,000
Total	200		21,800
Total			
Current	$1,000		8,800
Overdue	1,500		98,100

Exhibit 24.
Dollar days outstanding for two companies

$000's DRYAD CORP.

Receivables Category	Invoice Amount	Days Out-standing	Dollar Days
Current	$ 500	25	12,500
	400	18	7,200
	100	12	1,200
Total	1,000		20,900
30-day	200	48	9,600
	400	40	1,600
	200	34	6,800
Total	800		32,400
60-day	100	72	7,200
	300	65	19,500
	100	62	6,200
Total	500		32,900
90-day+	100	100	10,000
	100	92	9,200
Total	200		19,200
Total			
Current	$1,000		20,900
Overdue	1,500		84,500

Exhibit 24. *(Continued)*

- Griffen has more total dollar days in delinquent accounts than does Dryad ($98,100,000 versus $84,500,000).
- As a result, Griffen pays more to finance its receivables and has a greater exposure to bad debts.

CASH FLOW EFFECT

Dollar days outstanding analysis is a tool which can help you to evaluate and improve the cash flow from accounts receivable.

Consider first the situation with current accounts. Assuming that all customers paid their invoices when due, what would be the effect on cash flow if Dryad's greater current DDO level results from earlier billing?

Exhibit 25 analyzes this effect. It assumes that shipments for each of the amounts in current receivables was made at the same time for each company. But Dryad sent out invoices at the time of shipment, while Griffen delayed billing its customers. Cost of sales is 80 percent of selling price at each firm. All customers pay 30 days after being invoiced. Both firms pay 20 percent interest on funds used to finance receivables. The exhibit shows that because of its prompt invoicing, Dryad will enjoy a potential cash flow on current accounts that is $5,379 greater than Griffen's because of the lower carrying cost.

Next, it is possible to calculate the cash flow effect of having more dollar days in overdue accounts. This is determined by multiplying the overdue DDO from Exhibit 24 times the cost of sales times the cost of carrying receivables for one day (in this case .20/360). The calculations for each company are:

Griffen 98,100 × .80 × .20/360 = 43.6 = $43,600
Dryad   84,500 × .80 × .20/360 = 37.6 = $37,600
                                        $ 6,000

This indicates that Dryad will attain a $6,000 cash flow advantage from outstanding receivables in spite of the fact that its receivables appear exactly the same as Griffen's in the gross aging report.

GRIFFEN, INC.

Invoice Amount	Cost of Sales	Days Invoice Outstanding	Days Until Payment	Carrying Cost of Receivable
$500,000	$400,000	12	18	$4,000
400,000	320,000	6	24	4,267
100,000	80,000	4	26	1,156
			Total	$9,423

DRYAD CORP.

Invoice Amount	Cost of Sales	Days Invoice Outstanding	Days Until Payment	Carrying Cost of Receivable
$500,000	$400,000	25	5	$1,111
400,000	320,000	18	12	2,133
100,000	80,000	12	18	800
			Total	$4,044

Exhibit 25.
Cash flow effect of delayed invoicing

Dollar days analysis, then, can point out opportunities to improve collections and thus cash flows in cases where superficially the performance may seem adequate.

While a company with a large number of accounts may find that the dollar days approach involves a great quantity of calculations, the method can be programmed into the computer which handles the firm's accounting. From invoice and payment records already entered, the computer can easily generate regular, up-to-date DDO reports.

Dollar days reports may indicate impediments to cash flow in particular areas. For example, while total dollar days outstanding may remain the same, perhaps dollar days in the 30-day accounts have increased since the last report. This may mean that efforts to collect accounts are being delayed until they have been overdue for some time. By speeding up the initial collection efforts, the company can improve its cash flow.

ISOLATING THE VARIABLES

Dollar days analysis is one way to track receivables more carefully in order to determine the cash flow impact. But even without calculating the days outstanding for each invoice amount, a company can tell whether increased total receivables are the result of more sales or of poorer collection efforts. The example below shows how one company was able to evaluate collection efficiency using gross receivables figures.

WALTON PIPE CO.

The Walton Pipe Co. sells plumbing supplies to the construction industry. Its sales last year were $6 million.

Because the company experiences substantial fluctuation in sales levels from month to month and during its seasonally slower third quarter, Walton's accounts receivable manager found it difficult to accurately analyze receivables. In particular, he wanted to gain a better idea of whether an increase in total receivables was due to a sales increase in previous months, or whether it indicated that customers were paying their bills more slowly. Likewise, he wanted to be able to measure the effects of his efforts to improve the company's cash flow by improving collection performance.

His first step was to study the company's historical collection record to determine what its typical collection experience for a given three-month period had been. He looked at sales for each month in the period and calculated the amount of each month's sales that was still outstanding at the end of the period.

From this study, the manager calculated a target collection scenario. This is shown at the top of Exhibit 26. Sales are last year's

($000) Target	Sales	Receivables Outstanding	Receivables of Percent of Month's Sales	Weighted DSO
First Month	$ 500	$ 100	20%	6
Second Month	500	250	50	15
Third Month	500	450	90	27
Total	1,500	800		48
First Quarter				
Month 1	800	160	20	6
Month 2	1,000	600	60	18
Month 3	600	480	80	24
Total	2,400	1,240		48
Second Quarter				
Month 4	600	300	50	15
Month 5	300	210	70	21
Month 6	600	480	80	24
Total	1,500	990		60
Third Quarter				
Month 7	400	120	30	9
Month 8	300	180	60	18
Month 9	200	180	90	27
Total	900	480		54
Fourth Quarter				
Month 10	700	140	20	6
Month 11	600	240	40	12
Month 12	700	630	90	27
Total	2,000	1,010		45

Exhibit 26.
Target versus actual accounts receivables

HOW TO USE A WEIGHTED ANALYSIS TO IMPROVE CASH FLOW

annual sales averaged by month. Goals for the amount and percent of receivables still outstanding at the end of the period are set according to the past payment patterns of customers. While the company had not always collected receivables at this rate, the manager considered it to be a reasonable target that would produce a healthy cash flow, given the firm's business environment.

Weighted days sales outstanding is calculated by dividing the receivables outstanding for a given month by that month's average daily sales. Thirty-day months are assumed for convenience. For example, the average daily sales for the first months is $500/30 = $16.67. Weighted DSO is $100/16.67 = 6$. That means that at the end of the third month, 6 days' worth of first-month sales were still outstanding.

At the end of each quarter of the current year, the manager then compares his receivables situation to the standard. These comparisons are illustrated in Exhibit 26.

At the end of month 3, gross receivables from month 1 are 60 percent higher than the target. This increase, however, is the result of the substantially higher sales levels during the period.

In order to examine the results more thoroughly, however, the manager performs some calculations. First, he notes each month's change in weighted DSO in relation to the target. A higher percentage of month 2's sales are still in receivables, while month 3 shows a slightly better collection experience.

Next, he determines what portion of the total receivables increase is due to the higher level of sales. To do this, he calculates the difference in average daily sales between each month of the current quarter and the corresponding month of the target. He multiplies this difference by the target level of weighted DSO for that month.

For example, for month 1 the calculation is $(800/30 - 500/30) \times 6 = 60$. This means that $60,000 worth of total receivables due at the end of the quarter can be accounted for by the higher sales in month 1. For month 2, the calculation is $(1,000/30 - 500/30) \times 15 = 250$. Therefore, $250,000 worth of the receivables increase is the result of higher sales in month 2. He performs the same calculation for month 3. The results are seen in Exhibit 27.

($000)	Variation in Weighted DSO vs. Target	Increase in Total Receivables Due to Variation in Sales	Due to Variation in Collection
First Quarter			
Month 1	0	60	0
Month 2	3	250	100
Month 3	(3)	90	(60)
Total	0	400	40
Second Quarter			
Month 4	9	20	180
Month 5	6	(100)	60
Month 6	(3)	90	(60)
Total	12	10	180
Third Quarter			
Month 7	3	(20)	40
Month 8	3	(100)	30
Month 9	0	(270)	0
Total	6	(390)	70
Fourth Quarter			
Month 10	0	40	0
Month 11	(3)	50	(60)
Month 12	0	180	0
Total	(3)	270	(60)

Exhibit 27.
Analysis of variables in accounts receivable

Next, he determines whether changes in collection performance relative to the target have contributed to total receivables. This calculation involves multiplying average daily sales for the month in question times the variation in weighted DSO for that month.

For example, for month 2 the calculation is $1,000/30 \times 3 = 100$. This indicates that \$100,000 worth of total receivables for the quarter are the result of the slower receipt of payments for sales in month 2.

The collection experience for month 3 is calculated as follows: $600/30 \times (3) = (60)$. This means that total receivables have been reduced by \$60,000 due to the faster collection of month 3 accounts.

After making similar calculations for each month, the manager drew up a picture of receivables as seen in Exhibit 27. What he notices about the first quarter is that, of the \$440,000 increase in receivables, \$400,000 of the amount is due to higher sales while \$40,000 is the result of slightly slower collection of payments.

At the end of the second quarter, this situation has reversed itself. Almost all of the \$190,000 increase in receivables outstanding is the result of a less favorable collection experience. The manager realizes that this larger amount of cash tied up in receivables relative to sales is beginning to impede the company's overall cash flow. He begins a program during the next quarter to tighten credit and speed collections.

The results for the third quarter show two things. The first is that the manager's efforts to improve cash flow by speeding receivables collections is beginning to work. While total DSO are still not in line with the standard, they are at least improved in relation to the second quarter.

Also, an analysis of this quarter shows the value of the manager's detailed examination of receivables components. A less astute manager might point to the fact that total receivables have in fact dropped \$320,000 below the level set in the standard and think his collection efforts have paid off. The Walton manager, however, uncovers the fact that the quarter's low sales level more than accounts for the drop in receivables. He notes that payments slower than target levels still contribute \$70,000 to total receivables. If collection efforts are not improved further, the expected rebound in sales during the fourth quarter will again result in burgeoning receivables and a negative impact on cash flow.

Looking at the results of the fourth quarter, the manager sees that in spite of the fact that receivables are again higher than the target level, his efforts to improve cash flow have paid off. His analysis shows that the increase is entirely due to higher sales levels, and that faster customer payments have resulted in receivables being $60,000 less than they otherwise would have been.

CASH FLOW IMPACT

Increased sales always result in higher levels of accounts receivable. This is a factor not directly under the control of the accounts receivable manager. Collection efforts, though, can change. The Walton manager wanted to look at the direct cash flow impact of the company's collection experience as opposed to that resulting from sales variations.

The company's cost of sales was 80 percent of selling price. It was paying 22 percent interest to finance receivables. To determine the cash flow effect of collection efforts, the manager looked at the amount of receivables in excess of the target amount for each quarter that was attributable to collections. He multiplied this by 0.80 to find the cost of the receivables, then by 0.22/4 to find the quarterly impact on cash flow that resulted.

```
First Quarter    $ 40,000  × 0.80 × 0.22/4 = $ 1,760
Second Quarter  $180,000  × 0.80 × 0.22/4 =   7,920
Third Quarter   $ 70,000  × 0.80 × 0.22/4 =   3,080
Fourth Quarter  $(60,000) × 0.80 × 0.22/4 =  (2,640)
                                            $10,120
```

This indicates that Walton's collection experience resulted in a net $10,120 *reduction* in cash flow during the year compared to the target.

CASH FLOW ALERT

In order to clarify the technique, only the end of quarter analyses conducted by the Walton manager were used. In actual practice, you can use a rolling analysis to calculate each month. That is, at the end of March consider January, February, and March. At the end of April, take into account your receivables experience of February, March, and April. Each month will progress from first to third in its turn.

The Walton manager chose a quarterly analysis because almost all of its customers typically pay their bills within 90 days of sales. If you have different collection patterns, you can easily adapt this analysis to longer or shorter periods using the same methods.

8

MAKING THE CREDIT DECISION AND SETTING PAYMENT TERMS

Once a sale is made, its related cash flow impact is, to a great extent, out of your hands. You can request payment from the customer; you can cut off future credit sales to him; you can resort to a collection agency or legal action. But none of these tactics assures prompt payment of the original amount outstanding. During the time the customer withholds payment, your company's cash flow suffers: first, from the lack of cash represented by the sale; second, from the need to finance the amount of cash tied up in the products sold.

Better, then, to consider cash flow at a time when the matter is still under your control—during the credit decision phase. Credit decisions ultimately affect the amount of receivables outstanding, the length of time that customers take to pay bills, and the percentage of sales that wind up as bad debts.

Remember, though, that a balance is needed. Usually, when you refuse credit to a potential customer, you lose a sale. Overly severe credit standards can have as negative an impact on cash flow as excessively liberal ones.

TYBURN TOOL, LTD.

Tyburn Tool is a distributor of hand tools to retail hardware shops. Its credit manager decided to review current credit policy to determine if any changes were needed.

A large group of potential customers are willing to purchase Tyburn's products. Some are not as creditworthy as others. To simplify matters, the manager has divided all customers and potential customers into six groups, depending on the degree of risk perceived for each. For a given group, he estimates the total sales that Tyburn would gain if the company extended credit to the customers in question.

Using reports from credit agencies, financial data provided by the potential customers, industry studies, and Tyburn's own past experience with similar accounts, the credit manager estimates the rate of bad debts likely in each class, as well as the length of time customers in the group are likely to take, on average, to pay their bills. These classes are shown in Exhibit 28.

Tyburn currently sells to the three classes with the highest credit ratings, A, B, and C. Total sales amount to $1.4 million each year. Costs are 80 percent of the selling price. All sales are made on terms of net 30 days.

Class	Potential Sales	Expected Bad Debts as Percent of Sales	Expected Average Payment Period
A	$200,000	0.5%	30 days
B	400,000	1.0	30
C	800,000	2.5	35
D	600,000	5.0	40
E	400,000	8.0	50
F	500,000	9.0	60

Exhibit 28.
Classifying potential customers by risk

MAKING THE CREDIT DECISION AND SETTING PAYMENT TERMS

At this point, the manager could make the mistake of taking a purely profit-oriented view of his credit decision. That is to say, allowing for bad debts, will taking on a given class of customers increase Tyburn's gross profit?

Consider the situation if Tyburn began to sell to customers in class F. Looking only at the profit from sales, the result would be:

Incremental sales increase	$500,000
Cost of sales	400,000
Gross profit	100,000
Bad debts	45,000
Profit increase	$ 55,000

Since the sales would add $55,000 to Tyburn's annual profits even after allowing for bad debts, why not extend credit to this class of customers? And since classes D and E are even more creditworthy, the terms could be extended to them as well. Sales would more than double as a result and profits would increase.

EXAMINING THE CASH FLOW EFFECT

A profit analysis by itself, however, ignores the cash flow effect of the credit decision. From a cash flow perspective, taking on a new customer means making an investment. In addition to adding to sales, the new business adds to accounts receivable as well. And larger inventories have to be carried to service the additional accounts. The question is not just whether the company makes a profit from the customer's business. It's a matter of whether the profit justifies the amounts that have to be added to working capital.

Returning to customers in risk class F, then, a cash flow analysis shows a different picture. Tyburn maintains inventory that averages 73 days of sales. The annual cost of carrying that inventory amounts to 40 percent of its value. The cost of money used to finance receivables is estimated to be 25 percent annually.

Selling to customers in class F will require Tyburn to invest approximately $80,000 in additional inventory ($500,000 × 73/365 × 0.80). It will cost the company $32,000 each year to carry that inventory ($80,000 × 0.40).

The *cost* of daily sales to customers in this class will amount to $1,096 ($400,000/365). The credit manager uses the cost of receivables rather than the face amount because this gives a more accurate picture of Tyburn's actual investment.

Since the manager expects these customers to take an average of 60 days to pay, outstanding receivables will require a total investment of $65,760 ($1,096 × 60). Tyburn will have to pay $16,440 annually to finance these receivables ($65,760 × 0.25)).

The cash flow that can be expected from the account when these additional costs are taken into consideration is:

Incremental sales increase	$500,000
Cost of sales	400,000
Gross Profit	100,000
Bad debts	45,000
Inventory carrying cost	32,000
Accounts receivable carrying cost	16,438
Net incremental cash flow	$ 6,562

On the other hand, Tyburn will have to invest $80,000 in inventory and $65,753 in receivables, for a total working capital investment of $145,753. A simple calculation shows that the net incremental cash flow resulting from sales to these customers is only 4.5 percent of this increase in working capital. The credit manager might reasonably determine that extending credit to customers in class F is not a wise decision from a risk and cash flow point of view, even though sales to these customers would in fact add to Tyburn profits.

MAKING CREDIT DECISIONS

Tyburn's credit manager went on to conduct cash flow evaluations of all the classes of customers under consideration. These are shown in

Exhibit 29. In each case, the calculations involve the incremental increase in sales represented by the class.

Now the time comes to make the actual decisions about which classes to extend credit to. To do this, the manager must establish a target "return" on the investment the company will make in inventory and receivables if it extends credit to a given class.

Keep in mind when determining this standard that extending credit to customers is a relatively risky form of investment. The rate of return will materialize only if bad debts and receivable payment periods are accurate. A slight increase in bad debts or a delay in payments would have a negative impact on cash flow.

Part of the decision, then, will be based on the manager's confidence in his risk estimates. The more volatility he expects in actual bad debt and payment period results, the higher he should set his minimum return. Likewise, if customers in a class are diversified in terms of geography or business environment, then the risk would be lower than if they were more concentrated. An economic downturn would be less likely to affect all of them at once.

Tyburn's credit manager decided to extend credit to a class of customers only if the resulting cash flow expected was equal to at least 22 percent of the total investment in working capital. As a result, he chose to offer the 30-day credit terms to customers in class D, but not to those in classes E or F.

He then estimated the total cash flow that would result from the coming year's sales, including those to the customers in class D. As the following figures illustrate, by increasing its investment in working capital by $148,542 (from $324,882 to $473,424), Tyburn will realize a $600,000 sales increase and a $38,356 gain in net cash flow without incurring any unacceptable risks.

Current Situation

Sales		$1,400,000
Cost of sales		1,120,000
Gross profit		280,000
Bad debts		(25,000)
Average inventory	$224,000	

Inventory carrying cost		(89,600)
Average accounts receivable cost	100,822	
Accounts receivable carrying cost		(25,205)
Net cash flow		$ 140,195
Working capital investment	324,882	
Cash flow/working capital		43.2%

Situation with Class D Customers Added

Sales		$2,000,000
Cost of sales		1,600,000
Gross profit		400,000
Bad debts		(55,000)
Average inventory	320,000	
Inventory carrying cost		(128,000)
Average accounts receivable cost	153,424	
Accounts receivable carrying cost		$ (38,449)
Net cash flow		$ 178,551
Working capital investment	473,424	
Cash flow/working capital		37.7%

CASH FLOW ALERT

After you translate credit information into risk classes, you can adjust your credit policy to reflect the risk, economic conditions, and your capacity for production.

For example, class E customers in the preceding example were extended no credit at all and no sales to them were forecast. If you have capacity available, you might offer more stringent credit terms to class E customers such as 50 percent down when placing an order with the balance due 30 days after shipment. If there are a large number of potential customers in this class, some will place orders which will contribute something to overhead, profit, and cash flow.

MAKING THE CREDIT DECISION AND SETTING PAYMENT TERMS 103

	Class A	Class B	Class C
Sales	$200,000	$400,000	$800,000
Cost of sales	160,000	320,000	640,000
Gross profit	40,000	80,000	160,000
Bad debts	1,000	4,000	20,000
Average inventory	$32,000	$64,000	$128,000
Inventory carrying cost (@ 40%)	12,800	25,600	51,200
Average accounts receivable cost	13,151	26,301	61,370
Accounts receivable carrying cost (@ 25%)	3,288	6,575	15,342
Net cash flow	$ 22,914	$ 43,825	$ 73,485
Total working capital investment	$43,151	$90,301	$189,370
Cash flow/working capital	53.1%	48.5%	38.8%

Exhibit 29.
Evaluating credit risk and cash flows

	Class D	Class E	Class F
Sales	$600,000	$400,000	$500,000
Cost of sales	480,000	320,000	400,000
Gross profit	120,000	80,000	100,000
Bad debts	30,000	32,000	45,000
Average inventory	$ 96,000	$ 70,000	$ 80,000
Inventory carrying cost (@ 40%)	38,400	28,000	32,000
Average accounts receivable cost	52,602	43,836	65,753
Accounts receivable carrying cost (@ 25%)	13,151	10,959	16,438
Net cash flow	$ 38,449	$ 9,041	$ 6,562
Total working capital investment	$148,602	$113,836	$145,753
Cash flow/working capital	25.9%	7.9%	4.5%

Exhibit 29. *(Continued)*

CREDIT TERMS AND CASH FLOW

Credit terms and standards are the credit manager's tools for manipulating the cash flow impact of receivables.

More liberal terms—net 45 days, for example, instead of net 30 days—mean a larger proportion of assets tied up in receivables, higher carrying costs for receivables, and longer delays between sales and receipt of cash. Because they put less stringent demands on customers, liberal credit terms may also mean that the average customer's financial condition is less secure and that a higher proportion of bad debts will result.

Sales and credit terms vary inversely. Some potential customers will not be able to do business with your firm if terms are too stringent. Liberalizing terms means extending credit. This can increase sales at the expense of cash flow. Your goal is to achieve the optimum cash flow through careful adjustment of credit terms.

Competitive conditions, naturally, have a great influence on the terms your company offers. All trade credit serves as an inducement to buy. If your terms are more or less attractive than the norm of your industry, they will attract or repel customers.

If your product or service is in tight supply, you can afford to enforce strict credit terms or even demand cash payments, thereby maximizing cash flow. If you are operating in a hotly competitive market, however, you may have to offer liberal terms.

Discounts for early payment are a direct inducement to speed cash flow. You give up a small percentage of revenues in order to have cash on hand sooner after a sale. By doing so, you lower total receivables and lessen your exposure to bad debts.

In all considerations of credit terms, a careful study of the cash flow effects of the terms is essential. The cases below show how three companies handle credit terms.

SOUTHERN HOUSEWARES, INC.

Southern Housewares, Inc., manufactures plastic kitchen utensils. Customers are small distributors and retail chains. Southern's credit manager noticed that some potential customers were unable to meet Southern's terms of net payment in 30 days. After studying the matter, he estimated that if terms were lengthened to net 60 days, sales would increase by 10 percent.

Southern's current monthly sales average $450,000. Variable costs of sales average 85 percent of selling price. Because of late payments by some customers, receivables extend an average of 35 days. Bad debts average 1 percent of sales.

Southern turns its inventory twelve times a year. But because it purchases all materials on terms of net 30 and pays for them on time, the company essentially pays for inventory the day finished products are sold. Inventory carrying costs, therefore, are nil. The carrying cost for accounts receivable is 22 percent of the investment.

The credit manager further estimates that if Southern liberalized terms to net 60 days, the actual collection period would increase to 70 days. Bad debts, he figures, would grow to 1.5 percent of sales.

Exhibit 30 shows the manager's calculation of the cash flow effect of his proposal. Sales would be $45,000 higher. Gross profits would also be up. But the carrying cost of the additional receivables would reduce monthly cash flow by $9,818. In addition, bad debts would increase by an average of $2,925 each month.

The result: the manager's proposal would result in a $5,993 reduction in monthly cash flow, would increase the amount of capital invested in accounts receivable from $446,250 to $981,750, and would expose the company to greater risks. Clearly, the proposal should be rejected.

APEX CHEMICAL CORP.

One of this company's products is caustic soda. Monthly sales of the substance amount to an average of $200,000. The market is very competitive. Direct costs are 90 percent of sales.

Apex has always offered the standard industry credit terms of net 30 days. Recently, however, another company in the field has begun offering its customers the option of paying within 10 days and taking a 2 percent discount on the regular price. This arrangement is attrac-

MAKING THE CREDIT DECISION AND SETTING PAYMENT TERMS

SOUTHERN HOUSEWARES, INC.

	Current Situation (Terms: Net 30 Days)	Proposed Situation (Terms: Net 60 Days)
Monthly sales	$450,000	$495,000
Cost of sales	382,500	420,750
Gross monthly cash flow	67,500	74,250
Average accounts receivable cost	$446,250	$981,750
Monthly carrying cost (@ 22%)	8,181	17,999
Average monthly bad debts	4,500	7,425
Net cash flow	$ 54,819	$ 48,826

Exhibit 30.
Cash flow effect of increasing credit days

tive to some users of the product. A few Apex customers have requested similar terms.

The manager of the caustic soda division estimates that about 12 percent of the division's current customers will begin buying from its competitor if Apex doesn't offer the same terms. He further assumes that if he does make the discount available, about 60 percent of current customers will take advantage of it. Their payments would be outstanding no longer than 11 days. Among the 40 percent of customers who don't take advantage of the discount would be a larger proportion of slow-paying firms. Therefore, the manager figures that their receivables would extend 38 days on the average instead of the current average of 33 days.

Exhibit 31 illustrates the cash flow effects of the two options available to the Apex manager. In each case, the company maintains

APEX CHEMICAL CORP.

	Current Situation	Discount Not Offered	Discount Offered Customers Not Taking Discount	Discount Offered Customers Taking Discount
Monthly sales	$200,000	$176,000	$80,000	$120,000
Cost of sales	176,000	154,880	70,400	105,600
Discount	—	—	—	2,400
Gross cash flow	24,000	21,120	9,600	12,000
Average inventory	$ 58,667	$ 51,627	$ 23,467	$35,200
Monthly inventory carrying cost (@ 28%)	1,369	1,205	548	821
Average accounts receivable cost	193,600	170,368	89,173	38,720
			$112,640	$73,920
Monthly accounts receivable carrying cost (@ 18%)	2,904	2,556	1,338	581
			7,714	10,598
Net cash flow	$ 19,727	$ 17,359	(7,714+10,598)	$ 18,312
Working capital investment	$252,267	$221,995	(112,640+73,920)	$186,560

Exhibit 31.
Analyzing the effects of offering trade discounts

an inventory equal to 10 days sales. The carrying cost of the inventory is 28 percent while that of the accounts receivable is 18 percent. No bad debts are envisioned in either case.

The analysis shows that while the company's cash flow would not improve if the company were to go ahead and offer the discount, the resulting cash flow would still be nearly $1,000 a month greater than if sales declined as a result of retaining current terms.

In addition to the $953 monthly cash flow gain, three other facts also point toward offering the discount. First, Apex will retain market share for this product. Second, the total amount of assets tied up in inventory and receivables will be $35,435 less than it would be under the alternative situation. And third, because the discount will encourage a large portion of customers to pay early, Apex will have a lower exposure to possible bad debts.

BLAIR MANUFACTURING CO.

Blair Manufacturing makes ball bearings. Monthly sales are averaging $500,000. Because of a recession, the firm finds that its bad debts have risen to 3 percent of sales. And though it sells on terms of net 30 days, receivables now account for 44 days of sales.

Because the company is paying 26 percent to finance receivables, the Blair credit manager is concerned about the situation. He has proposed a plan under which credit would not be extended to any customer whose debt was more than twice its net worth. He estimates that this would reduce sales by about 8 percent. But since these customers are the slowest paying and generate the largest proportion of bad debts, the action would reduce receivables to 36 DSO and lower bad debts to 1.5 percent of sales.

As with Southern Housewares, Blair maintains an average of one month's sales in inventory. But it buys its materials at net 30, so inventory costs are not a consideration.

Exhibit 32 gives the manager's calculations of the cash flow results of tightening credit. Though sales and gross profits are lower, monthly cash flow increases by $3,243. In addition, the decrease in accounts receivable outstanding would mean that Blair would have an

BLAIR MANUFACTURING CO.

	Current Situation	Proposed Situation
Monthly sales	$500,000	$460,000
Cost of sales	400,000	368,000
Gross cash flow	100,000	92,000
Average accounts receivable cost	$586,667	$441,600
Accounts receivable carrying cost (@ 26%)	12,711	9,568
Average monthly bad debts	15,000	6,900
Net cash flow	$ 72,289	$ 75,532

Exhibit 32.
Cash flow effect of tightening credit terms

additional $145,067 to use for other purposes. The manager decides that the more stringent credit standards are a good idea.

NEED FOR REALISTIC ASSUMPTIONS

It is important to keep in mind in making cash flow projections related to credit terms that the calculations rest on assumptions. The accuracy of the analysis will be no more accurate than that of these assumptions.

In the case of Southern Housewares, for example, the manager is assuming that sales will grow by 10 percent if terms are made more liberal. If the additional sales do not materialize, then the cash flow computations will not be correct. Likewise, if receivables stretch out beyond the projected 70 days, cash flow will also suffer. The same thing will happen if bad debts amount to a higher proportion of sales than the one anticipated. Note that similar assumptions and estimates are made in the other two cases.

Because cash flow projections rest on the foundation of these assumptions, it is important to base them on the best data available. Often, your own company's records of past experience will provide the best guide. Commercial credit reporting agencies can also supply historical data and estimates.

Furthermore, you must try to foresee any additional factors that will affect cash flow. By instituting a discount for early payment, for example, Apex Chemical may incur additional accounting and administrative costs. In order to enforce its stiffer credit standards, Blair Manufacturing may have to spend cash on more detailed credit reports on its customers. If these costs can be quantified, you should include them in the cash flow analysis.

CASH FLOW ALERT

A sales forecast should be more than an optimistic hope. Inaccurate sales forecasts are a prime cause of either obsolete inventories or of production inefficiencies caused by last minute rush orders. Both results strain cash flow. The sales department must continually strive for more accurate forecasts in order to facilitate the optimum inventory levels and production scheduling. Significant changes in sales levels should be rapidly communicated to everyone concerned, including inventory and purchasing managers. Computerized sales projections are now feasible for almost any size firm. They not only give all managers up to date data, but significantly reduce paperwork.

9

HOW TO EVALUATE YOUR CUSTOMERS TO MAXIMIZE CASH FLOW

Bad debts and slow payment of bills are the two main dangers to cash flow that can be avoided by making effective credit decisions. Therefore, avoiding these dangers by deciding which customers are good credit risks is an important part of protecting cash flow.

Keep in mind a key principle: From a cash flow point of view, the best customer is not necessarily the one who buys the most. Sales-oriented companies, greedy for increased revenues, often take on customers who contribute a great deal to sales volume but very little to cash flow.

THE CASH FLOW IMPACT OF CREDIT RISKS

Consider the case of Greenville Electronics Co. Two of the firm's customers are Norris Corporation and Foxton, Inc. Foxton is the more highly regarded account since this customer does twice the volume with Greenville each year compared to Norris. However, because of its own tight cash flow, Foxton takes an average of 90 days to pay its bills, while Norris pays promptly in 10 days.

	Norris Corporation	Foxton, Inc.
Monthly sales	$30,000	$ 60,000
Cost of sales (85% of price)	25,500	51,000
Gross profit	4,500	9,000
Investment in inventory	$51,000	$102,000
Monthly inventory carrying cost	1,700	3,400
Average accounts receivable investment	8,500	153,000
Monthly accounts receivable carrying cost	170	3,060
Net monthly cash flow	$ 2,630	$ 2,540
Net annual cash flow	$31,560	$ 30,480
Working capital investment	$59,500	$255,000

Exhibit 33.
Cash flow evaluation of customers

Exhibit 33 illustrates the cash flow that Greenville derives from each customer. Greenville carries an average inventory equal to 60 days of sales at an annual cost of 40 percent of the value of the inventory. Its carrying cost for receivables is 24 percent.

Foxton, because of its slower rate of paying bills, actually produces a lower rate of cash flow than Norris. In fact, while Norris returns a healthy 53 percent on Greenville's required investment in working capital after all costs, Foxton produces a meager 12 percent.

But bad debts can have an even more devastating effect on cash flow. Exhibit 34 shows what happened when another of Greenville's customers, Brown Manufacturing, went bankrupt. This customer failed to pay Greenville for $57,375 worth of products. The result? Nearly two years' cash flow from the customer was negated. In fact, a negative cash flow of $20,751 resulted from the account over the course

	Brown Manufacturing Co.	
Monthly sales		$ 45,000
Cost of sales		38,250
Gross profit		6,750
Average inventory	$76,500	
Monthly inventory carrying cost		2,550
Average receivables investment (45 days sales)	57,375	
Monthly carrying cost		1,148
Net monthly cash flow		$ 3,052
Net annual cash flow		$ 36,624
Bad debt loss		$ 57,375
Net annual cash flow after loss		$(20,751)

Exhibit 34.
The cash flow effect of a bad debt

of the year, and inventory of $76,500 became an excess investment.

It is clear from these examples that sales and credit managers must look beyond the profitability of a customer's account in making an evaluation. They must attempt to reduce bad debts to a point where they do not represent a serious threat to cash flow. And they must carefully assess sales to slow-paying customers who cause receivables to drag out to unacceptable lengths.

TIMING OF CASH FLOWS

Before evaluating customers to assure a healthy cash flow, note one mistake that companies often make. They focus too much on the potential customer's financial health and not enough on their own.

A company which has abundant cash, a steady flow of incoming funds, and few pressing financial obligations would not necessarily make the same credit decisions as a firm which is cash poor and hard pressed to meet its required payments.

The examples in Exhibit 35 illustrate this point. They represent the monthly cash budgets for two similar companies. Both have the same sales and profit margins. But while their situations are similar, their cash flows are not. Company A has a higher debt and must make regular interest payments. It also has to pay an installment on its bank loan. And it is planning a needed investment in new equipment. Company B, on the other hand, has fewer financial obligations.

($000's) Company A	January	February	March
Monthly cash receipts	$500	$500	$500
Cost of sales	400	400	400
Cash flow from operations	100	100	100
Beginning cash	50	110	150
Interest payments	40	40	40
Loan installments	—	—	200
Capital expenditures	—	100	—
Ending cash	$110	$150	$ 10

Company B	January	February	March
Monthly cash receipts	$500	$500	$500
Cost of sales	400	400	400
Cash flow from operations	100	100	100
Beginning cash	100	180	260
Interest payments	20	20	20
Loan installments	—	—	—
Capital expenditures	—	—	—
Ending cash	$180	$260	$340

Exhibit 35.
The timing of cash flows on credit decisions

HOW TO EVALUATE YOUR CUSTOMERS TO MAXIMIZE CASH FLOW

How do the respective conditions of these companies affect credit decisions? Managers at company A realize that they are much more susceptible to bad debt and slow payment effects. As a result, they are likely to extend credit more conservatively than the managers at company B.

To see the justification for this, consider the effect on each company if during March half of its customers begin paying their bills a month later than usual. For company B this means a greater investment in receivables but no immediate cash flow problems. As Exhibit 36 illustrates, though, company A experiences a much more serious problem. A $240,000 cash shortage develops immediately. The firm

($000's)

Company A	January	February	March
Monthly cash receipts	$500	$500	$250
Cost of sales	400	400	400
Cash flow from operations	100	100	(150)
Beginning cash	50	110	150
Interest payments	40	40	40
Loan installments	—	—	200
Capital expenditures	—	100	—
Ending cash	$110	$150	$(240)

Company B	January	February	March
Monthly cash receipts	$500	$500	$250
Cost of sales	400	400	400
Cash flow from operations	100	100	(150)
Beginning cash	100	180	260
Interest payments	20	20	20
Loan installments	—	—	—
Capital expenditures	—	—	—
Ending cash	$180	$260	$ 90

Exhibit 36.
Effect on cash of delays in customer payments

either has to curtail operations, delay repaying its bank loan, or seek emergency financing.

The question to ask, then, is not simply how solvent are potential customers, but how much risk can your own company take on? If expected bad debts materialize, will they disrupt operations? Can you obtain financing to cover receivables if customers' accounts drag out? Do you risk a cash shortage as well as higher carrying costs?

LOOKING AT PRODUCT MIX

Just as your financial and cash flow situation should be taken into account before you look at potential customers' credit worthiness, so should you look at the product mix that the customer will be purchasing from you. If a customer will be buying a product with a high profit margin, then you can afford to take on the account without endangering cash flow even if the firm is a greater credit risk. However, higher standards should be established for customers purchasing only low-margin items.

One quick way to determine whether a client is a safe risk is to use the following formula:

$$M(1-P) - C > (FP) + C$$

where:

M = gross profit margin on products sold to customer
P = probability of bad debt (expressed as decimal)
F = cost of goods sold
C = carrying cost of inventory, accounts receivable to support customer's business

For example, a customer purchases $10,000 worth of goods annually. The profit margin is 20 percent. The cost of carrying inventory and accounts receivable amounts to 6 percent of the selling price. Examining the customer's credit history and financial situation, you estimate the risk of bad debts at 5 percent.

Your calculation would be:

$$\$2{,}000\,(1 - .05) - \$600 > \$8{,}000 \times .05 + \$600$$
$$\$1{,}300 > \$1{,}000$$

The formula indicates that taking on the customer's business would be feasible from a cash flow perspective.

But now assume this same customer wants to purchase a different product line, on which your gross margin is only 15 percent. Again you apply the formula to test whether you are justified in extending credit:

$$\$1{,}500\,(1 - .05) - \$600 > \$8{,}500 \times .05 + \$600$$
$$\$825 > \$1{,}025$$

The calculation indicates that you should not offer credit to the customer in this case. The risk of a bad debt loss is not justified by the resulting cash flow from his business. Note that this is the case even though the customer's financial situation has not changed.

PROFIT MARGINS AND CREDIT POLICY

To see in more detail how product mix should affect credit decisions, consider the example illustrated in Exhibit 37. The Delmar Corporation consists of two divisions. Its Electrograph Division sells custom-designed electronic components and enjoys a profit margin of 40 percent of sales. The Chemco Division sells commodity chemicals with a margin of only 10 percent.

Listed first are last year's results and the cash flow from each division. While the Chemco Division produces significantly less cash on the same amount of sales, its 22 percent rate of return on inventory and receivables investments is still greater than Delmar's target goal of 20 percent. The Electrograph Division more than pays for the company's working capital investment in a single year.

Consider, however, what happens if the two divisions apply the same credit standards to evaluating customers. First, look at the sit-

($000's)	Electrograph Division		Chemco Division	
Sales	$4,000		$4,000	
Cost of sales	2,400		3,600	
Gross profit	1,600		400	
Average inventory	$400		$400	
Inventory carrying cost	(@40%)	160	(@30%)	120
Average accounts receivable cost outstanding (45 days sales)	300		450	
Carrying cost (20%)		60		90
Net cash flow		$1,380		$ 190
Working capital investment		$ 700		$ 850
Cash flow/working capital		197%		22%
Effect of 2% Bad Debts				
Cash flow		$1,380		$ 190
Bad debts		80		80
Net cash flow		$1,380		$ 110
Net cash flow/working capital		186%		13%
Effect of 90-day Average Receivables				
Gross profit		$1,600		$ 400
Inventory carrying cost		160		120
Average accounts receivable cost outstanding (90 days sales)	600		900	
Carrying cost (20%)		120		180
Net cash flow		$1,320		$ 100
Working capital investment		$1,000		$1,300
Cash flow/working capital		132%		7.7%

Exhibit 37.
Profit margins and cash flows

uation if the divisions adopt credit standards that result in a total bad debt experience of 2 percent of sales. Net cash flow at both divisions is reduced by $80,000.

At Electrograph, this represents only a 6 percent reduction in cash flow. But at Chemco, cash flow falls by 42 percent and the return on the company's working capital investment drops to 13 percent, an unacceptable rate based on the 20 percent goal.

Next, look at the effects of slower customer payments. Normally, customers at both divisions take an average of 45 days to pay their bills. What if more-liberal credit standards result in receivables that average 90 days of sales? Electrograph's cash flow still remains acceptable. But at Chemco, cash flow is cut almost in half. The new cash flow represents only a 7.7 percent return on the now larger investment in inventory and receivables. This is certainly a situation that Chemco managers want to avoid.

The solution, clearly, is for each division to set its credit policy based on its own margins and cash flow situation. Electrograph can afford to expand its sales base by taking on customers with lower credit ratings and longer payment practices. Chemco, however, needs to sell only to customers with little chance of increasing bad debts and must maintain stricter limits on the length of its receivables.

When customers are neatly grouped according to divisions, as they are at Delmar, setting differential credit standards is easy. But at many firms, products with different profit margins are grouped together. A company may sell hundreds of different products, each with a different margin.

To make evaluation easier, group products into categories with similar rates of gross profit. When considering a new customer, determine which products it is interested in purchasing. Take that product mix into account when deciding how much credit to extend.

For example, you might be offering three classes of products: class 1 with a 35 percent average gross margin; class 2 with a 28 percent margin; and class 3 with 15 percent. If the product mix that a new customer wants to buy includes primarily class 1 products, you can afford to be more liberal in your evaluation than if it is interested mainly in class 3 items.

EVALUATING A POTENTIAL CUSTOMER

Just as correct credit decisions are an important factor affecting your company's cash flow, the potential customer's own cash flow situation should be a vital consideration in making those decisions.

Certainly you will also look at its profitability and financial structure. Has the potential customer shown a steady increase in net earnings? Have earnings remained a comparable percent of sales? Is the firm highly leveraged? Does it have bank loans coming due?

But ultimately, you are interested in whether the company can pay its bills on time. That requires it to have an adequate cash flow.

The applications of cash flow are also important. Every company incurs necessary and discretionary expenses. If a potential customer's cash from operations is taken up by high-priority payments like interest and debt installments, it is more likely to face a cash shortage than the company which spends its available cash on research or other optional outlays.

Exhibit 38 gives the cash flow picture for the most recent year of two firms which have applied to your company for trade credit. Sales at both companies are the same. Profitability is similar. But the cash flow situations are very different.

Barton Processing, for example, shows a significantly higher flow of cash from operations and higher net cash flow than does Afton Manufacturing. In addition, Barton applies most of its cash flow to discretionary spending such as research, capital expenditures, and dividends. The majority of Afton's cash, however, goes to pay interest and repay loans.

Consider, then, what would happen if both firms encountered a sales slump which cut cash flows. Barton could probably weather the slump and keep paying its suppliers. It could cut back first on research and capital spending. And it could cut its dividend to shareholders. Afton, on the other hand, facing demands from its banks, might have to preserve its cash flow by slowing down or omitting payments to suppliers. In an extreme case, the firm might even fail to meet those obligations.

These facts should be taken into account when deciding whether or not to extend credit to each firm and in setting a credit limit.

($000's)	Barton Processing	Afton Manufacturing
Sales	$2,000	$2,000
Increase in accounts receivable	20	22
Cash inflow	$1,980	$1,978
Cost of goods sold	1,485	1,500
General and administrative expenses	140	160
Selling expenses	50	52
Taxes	60	54
Inventory increase	60	75
Accounts payable increase	(26)	(30)
Cash outflows	$1,769	$1,811
Operating cash flow	$ 211	$ 167
Interest expense	12	50
Debt repayment	30	90
Research and development	45	—
Capital expenditures	60	—
Dividends	20	—
Total nonoperating expenditures	$ 167	$ 140
Net cash flow	$ 44	$ 27

Exhibit 38.
Cash flow effects of discretionary spending

Keep in mind, however, that cash flow can be affected by many factors. Assume a firm is experiencing rapid growth. Investments in capital equipment, inventories, and receivables can produce substantial negative cash flows during a given period. Yet, if the firm is profitable and has an adequate depth of financial backing from its bank or investors, it may still represent a good credit risk as a customer.

RISK CLASSIFICATION

A system of risk classification for all customers and potential customers allows you to more easily handle credit decisions and set credit terms. The number of categories will depend on the range of customers your company considers and its needs for refinement.

The criteria for including a company in a given class will also vary according to the industries and business environments with which your company deals. The criteria should be objective and relatively easy to monitor.

Exhibit 39 shows a simple risk classification system set up by Helical Design Company. Note that trends in profitability are as important a part of the standard as is absolute profitability.

Risk Category	Current Ratio $\left(\dfrac{\text{Current Assets}}{\text{Current Liabilities}}\right)$	Debt	Profitability Trend
1	1.5+	Less than 50% of net worth	15%+ average growth in operating earnings past 3 years
2	1.3+	Less than 75% of net worth	10%+ average growth
3	1.0+	Less than 150% of net worth	Less than 10% growth
4	Less than 1	More than 150%	Decline in operating earnings
5	Less than 1	More than 250%	Decline in operating earnings

Exhibit 39.
Classifying customers by risk

Risk classification can be used to monitor the total risk that your company faces from its customers. For example, though Helical extends credit to a wide variety of customers, management has decided that customers in risk categories 3 through 5 should not account for more than 50 percent of sales. Exhibit 40 shows how the company monitored these risk categories during a recent year. Because managers observed that risk had exceeded the standard during the second quarter, tighter credit limits were introduced during the third quarter. This brought the distribution within acceptable limits.

CREDIT EVALUATION REPORT

In addition to its classification system, Helical keeps on file a credit evaluation report for each customer. This form contains the information that the credit manager uses to determine the terms and amount of trade credit to extend to a customer.

Exhibit 41 shows a credit report on the Western Supply Co., one of Helical's customers. Such a report is updated at least annually. It would be changed more often if Western experienced a significant change in its financial situation. The credit manager reviews the form whenever Western requests additional credit or different terms.

Exhibit 42 is a blank report that you can reproduce and use in evaluating your own customers.

($000's)

Risk Class	First Quarter Sales	% of Total	Second Quarter Sales	% of Total	Third Quarter Sales	% of Total	Fourth Quarter Sales	% of Total
1	$ 356	14.0	$ 229	9.6	$ 388	18.9	$ 400	19.6
2	934	36.6	646	27.0	746	36.4	972	47.6
3	782	30.7	862	36.0	610	29.7	399	19.5
4	375	14.7	411	17.1	255	12.4	210	10.3
5	103	4.0	249	10.4	52	2.5	62	3.0
Total	$2,550		$2,051		$2,397		$2,043	
% of Total Sales in Risk Classes 3–5		49.4		63.5		44.6		32.8

Exhibit 40.
Analysis of sales by risk class

CREDIT EVALUATION FORM

($000's)

Date __5/84__

Customer __Western Supply Co.__
Address __220 S. Singer St.__
Phone __990-3456__

Credit Class __3__
Credit Limit __300__

Our Sales Past Year

Category A	500	Margin	28%
Category B	80	Margin	21%
Category C	—	Margin	18%
Total	580		

Current Amount Outstanding __120__
Past Due __20__

Financial Data as of __3/84__

Current Assets __2520__   Current Ratio __1.2__
Current Liabilities __2140__

Working Capital __380__
Fixed Assets __2400__
Deferred Liabilities __780__

Net Worth __2000__

Debt Due (less than 5 years) __1900__

Annual Sales __8500__

Operating Income __850__

Average change in Operating
Income (past 3 years) __+8%__

Net Income __500__

Depreciation & Amortization __400__
Net Cash Flow __900__

Comments: _____

Exhibit 41.
Sample credit evaluation form

CREDIT EVALUATION FORM

($000's)

Date _____

Customer _____ Credit Class _____
Address _____ Credit Limit _____
Phone _____

Our Sales Past Year

    Category A _____ Margin _____
    Category B _____ Margin _____
    Category C _____ Margin _____

    Total _____

Current Amount Outstanding _____
    Past Due _____

Financial Data as of _____

    Current Assets _____ Current Ratio _____
    Current Liabilities _____

    Working Capital _____
    Fixed Assets _____
    Deferred Liabilities _____

    Net Worth _____

    Debt Due (less than 5 years) _____

    Annual Sales _____

    Operating Income _____

    Average change in Operating
      Income (past 3 years) _____

    Net Income _____

    Depreciation & Amortization _____
    Net Cash Flow _____

    Comments: _____

Exhibit 42.
Sample credit evaluation form

10

CASH FLOW AND CAPITAL SPENDING

Rondack Electrical Co., a hypothetical manufacturer of components for light motors, currently uses $7,500 worth of screws each year. A supervisor in the assembly department has suggested that it make its own screws, which would save money and increase profit. He has investigated the matter and found that an appropriate machine would cost $20,000. He has further calculated that, taking into account the cost of the screw stock that the company would have to purchase, plus the upkeep on the machine and other factors, Rondack would be able to generate a cash flow of $5,000 yearly.

Still, $20,000 represents a substantial outlay for a small company like Rondack. Is the investment worth it? To find out, the supervisor makes another calculation—he finds the payback period. The formula he uses is:

$$\text{Payback period} = \frac{\text{Initial outlay}}{\text{Annual cash benefit}}$$

The payback period for the screw machine would be

$$\text{Payback period} = \frac{\$20,000}{\$\ 5,000} = 4 \text{ years}$$

Thus, the company would recoup the cost of the machine in four years.

What does this analysis tell the supervisor? First, it indicates that the payback period is shorter than the useful life of the machine, which its manufacturer lists as ten years. Second, it indicates that the investment is probably sound. While the machine won't pay for itself during the first year, or even the first three years that it is in operation, it will repay its cost in four years, which will leave another six years of cash flow benefits.

But the payback period tells the supervisor something else. Because the payback is not immediate, the company will have cash at risk during those years. Its cash resources will be reduced during that time. This is the primary role of payback analysis in relation to cash flow: it tells the manager the length of time that it will take to restore the company to the original cash position.

The payback period can be used to compare two projects as to their effect on the company's cash pool. For example, suppose another of Rondack's managers proposes the purchase of a materials handling system also costing $20,000. Labor savings are projected to cut costs, producing a net cash gain each year according to the following schedule:

Year	Cash Benefit	Cumulative Cash Benefit
1	$8,000	$ 8,000
2	5,000	13,000
3	4,000	17,000
4	2,000	19,000
5	2,000	21,000

When the yearly cash flows from the project are not equal, the payback period can be calculated easily from the cumulative cash benefits. The materials handling system in this example will have repaid its initial cost during the fifth year. To find the exact payback period, assume that the cash flow in that year is uniform and interpolate by dividing the cash needed to make the cumulative flow equal to the cost by the cash flow for the entire year. Therefore, the payback period is:

$$\text{Payback period} = 4 \text{ years} + \frac{\$1,000}{\$2,000} = 4.5 \text{ years}$$

According to this analysis, then, the screw machine would be a better investment for Rondack because it will pay back its investment in a shorter period of time.

WHEN TO USE PAYBACK PERIOD

While sophisticated financial analysts find that the payback period approach lacks the refinement of more complex analytical techniques, it still remains a valuable tool for the ordinary manager. It is particularly useful for companies that wish to promote cash awareness among managers. It is equally important when a company is short of cash, credit, or both. In such cases, managers must take into consideration the degree of commitment that any capital project involves. Payback period provides a convenient device for measuring that commitment.

Payback period is also useful for low-cost capital projects where spending and expected cash inflows are relatively simple to calculate. It can likewise help the company that is facing an unstable business climate. For example, a toy manufacturing company was choosing between two product lines. Both required the purchase of dedicated injection molding machinery. One project would repay its costs in two years, the other in 3.4 years.

Because the toy industry was so influenced by trends from one year to the next, the firm rejected the 3.4-year project as too risky. A payback period of two years was the maximum acceptable, given the rapid changes that could affect the market. This principle also applies to any industry affected by style and fashion. An apparel company would not want to invest cash in custom machinery to produce a currently popular line of goods if the payback period was projected at five years. The popularity of the item could disappear long before then. The same holds true in industries with rapidly developing technologies. Some electronic and semiconductor components represent the "state of the art" for less than a year. Capital investment dedicated to these products must have a rapid payback.

APPLYING PAYBACK ANALYSIS

Payback period analysis must be applied with common sense. For example, what if Rondack managers were comparing the screw machine project to a packaging machine that would produce the same $5,000 annual cash savings and cost only $15,000? The payback period for the packaging machine is shorter, three years versus four years for the screw machine. But the packaging machine has a useful life of only five years compared to the ten-year life of the screw machine. The total payback for the screw machine will be $50,000, while that of the packaging machine will be only $25,000. This aspect of the investment must be taken into account along with the payback analysis. The company's choice of projects will depend, among other things, on how much cash is currently available to spend on capital goods.

The timing of cash flows must also be considered. For example, there are two projects, each requiring an initial outlay of $75,000. The projected cash benefits of each project are:

Year	Project A	Project B
1	$50,000	$10,000
2	20,000	20,000
3	5,000	45,000

Both projects pay for themselves in three years. But project A clearly involves less risk to the company's cash position because the bulk of the funds spent are paid back in the first year. The fact that the projects have equal payback periods shouldn't disguise this fact. But look, too, at the subsequent cash benefits of the projects:

Year	Project A	Project B
4	$5,000	$15,000
5	5,000	10,000
6	5,000	8,000

CASH FLOW AND CAPITAL SPENDING   133

Project B will pay back more cash over the six-year period, but project A puts money in the company's coffers more quickly. Which project is preferable if the company's cash is limited? This requires careful consideration of a variety of factors. The more detailed analytical techniques discussed in this chapter can also help weigh the advantages of competing projects.

THE BAILOUT FACTOR

All investments involve a degree of risk. A market can dry up, materials can become more costly, competition can increase. The manager focusing on the cash flow aspects of capital spending will often want to consider contingencies. What if the investment proves to be no longer viable? How much can the company recoup if it has to bail out of the project? Here, the salvage value of the purchased equipment or facility becomes important and must be considered along with the payback analysis.

For example, a department manager in a company making components for the aircraft industry was considering two systems to speed up shipments and cut labor costs. One alternative was to purchase several forklift trucks. The other was to install a conveyor system. Both projects would cost $40,000 and have ten-year useful lives. The trucks would produce cash benefits of $10,000 each year. The conveyor system would cut costs by $12,000. An ordinary payback analysis shows that the conveyor system would repay its cost earlier, in 3.3 years, versus four years for the forklift trucks.

The market for the aircraft components, though, was highly volatile. The company wanted to know what would happen if the product line for which the capital improvements were intended had to be abandoned during the first few years. The manager knew that the forklift trucks had a relatively high salvage value on the secondhand market. The conveyor system, custom built for this application, would not be worth much if sold or scrapped. To calculate the bailout factor, the manager added the estimated salvage value of the systems to the cumulative cash savings:

FORKLIFT TRUCKS

Year	Cumulative Cash Benefit	Salvage Value	Total (Bailout Value)
1	$10,000	$25,000	$35,000
2	20,000	20,000	40,000
3	30,000	15,000	45,000
4	40,000	10,000	50,000

Conveyor System

1	$12,000	$ 8,000	$20,000
2	24,000	6,000	30,000
3	36,000	4,000	40,000
4	48,000	2,000	50,000

This calculation shows that while the regular payback period is longer for the forklift trucks, they represent less of a risk to cash flow because after the second year the original cost of the machinery would be covered in the event of a bailout. The conveyor system does not reach this point until the end of the third year.

Naturally, if the need for the bailout were very unlikely, the more rapid cash inflows from the conveyor system would make it the more attractive investment. But the bailout factor is worth calculating when cash is especially tight and the proposed investments especially risky. It should be considered when judging custom-designed machinery, projects with heavy installation or building costs, leases with large buy-out provisions, and other projects with high up-front cash commitments.

DEPRECIATION AND TAXES

Depreciation expense is not taken into account in any cash flow analysis of the return on capital spending because it is purely an accounting concept. It spreads the cost of an investment, for accounting purposes, over a number of years. Cash flow analysis requires that the capital cost be recognized when it is incurred, usually at the beginning of the project.

Therefore, always eliminate depreciation expense from your cash flow calculations. For example, you are contemplating spending $100,000 on a machine to produce a product which will yield $15,000 in increased earnings. But the machine will be depreciated on the company's books at $10,000 per year. The actual cash flow benefit, therefore, will be $25,000 (the $15,000 in earnings and the $10,000 in depreciation that your company's accounts will have subtracted to calculate earnings). Payback and other cash flow calculations should follow this approach.

Depreciation, however, does have an effect on the cash benefits of a project because of the extent to which it reduces income taxes. For example, if a company is paying 40 percent of income to taxes, then the $10,000 of depreciation will yield a cash benefit (in lower taxes) of $4,000. While the depreciation expense itself is not included in the cash flow, the cash benefit is.

The income tax consequences of capital spending are an important consideration and should not be overlooked. They are also complicated, varying according to tax rates, income and spending levels, depreciation methods, etc. Managers should consult the company controller or financial staff for advice on how to include tax factors into capital spending proposals. The following points will illustrate some of the issues involved:

- Tax can affect both the total amount of cash flow and its timing.
- Tax avoidance and the resulting enhanced cash flow is part of a manager's responsibility.
- Besides straight-line depreciation (the cost of the item divided by the number of years in its useful life), two forms of accelerated depreciation are in common use: the sum-of-the-years digits (SYD) and the double-declining balance (DDB) methods.
- Cash flow is always enhanced by accelerated depreciation and a manager should normally choose the earliest deduction possible.
- Special tax benefits, such as an investment tax credit, can further influence the cash consequences of investments.

- Capital gains treatment, loss carryforwards, definition of capital assets, exempt income, and many other factors can affect the tax treatment of capital spending. When in doubt, consult your tax experts.

Net present value analysis (NPV) is a method of discounting the projected cash flows from an investment in order to take into consideration the return on the investment. The basis of NPV is the hurdle rate of interest. This rate, determined by a company's financial managers, will usually be somewhat higher than the cost of borrowing money. Because of risk factors and the company's goals for return on investment, it may be considerably higher.

The net present value calculations compare the future cash flows to the present expenditure. Once the hurdle rate is chosen, the cash flow for each year is discounted by the appropriate present value factor (see appendix). The present values of the cash flows for all the years are added together. From this sum is subtracted the initial cost of the project. The result is the net present value.

If the net present value amount is zero, it means that the return on the project equals the hurdle rate and that the investment is acceptable. If the NPV is positive, the return on investment is more attractive than the hurdle rate because the project will generate additional cash. If the NPV is negative, however, the project will not generate enough cash to meet the hurdle rate and be rejected.

The table on page 137 shows how Rondack's manager applied net present value analysis to his decision about the screw machine (his company's controller had set the hurdle rate at 15 percent).

The positive net present value tells the manager that the project is worthwhile under the present circumstances and assumptions. The analysis also allows the manager to consider contingencies. What if interest rates skyrocketed and the hurdle rate had to be raised to 20 percent? New discount factors can be substituted and the NPV recalculated, each year's cash flow being reduced in terms of present value. What if the cash inflows were only $4,500 instead of $5,000? What if the useful life of the equipment were six years instead of ten? Each of these changes can be calculated, with a new NPV indicating the viability of the project based on the assumptions.

Year	Present Value Factor (@ 15% Hurdle)	Actual Cash Inflow	Present Value of Cash Inflow
1	.870	$5,000	$ 4,350
2	.756	5,000	3,780
3	.658	5,000	3,290
4	.572	5,000	2,860
5	.497	5,000	2,485
6	.432	5,000	2,160
7	.376	5,000	1,880
8	.327	5,000	1,635
9	.284	5,000	1,420
10	.247	5,000	1,235
		Total present value	$25,095
		Initial cost	(20,000)
		Net present value	$ 5,095

CASH FLOW ALERT

A useful shortcut in calculating NPV when the cash flows from each period are equal, is to add the present value factors over the life of the project. For example, the present value factors in the example under discussion add up to 5.019. This figure can be used to compare different cash flow amounts. For instance, if the cash flow each year is only $4,000, then the total present value of the project is $4,000 × 5.019 = $20,076; and the net present value is $76 (indicating that the project still passes the hurdle rate).

USING NET PRESENT VALUE

Net present value analysis gives a more comprehensive look at cash flow implications of capital investments than does payback period. It is best used for longer-term projects where the cost of capital is increasingly important. This applies both to projects requiring outside financing and to those that use only internal funds. NPV is a useful tool for the manager because it is relatively easy to calculate, leaves the decision about the hurdle rate to financial experts, and gives a clear "go/no go" financial indication about the intended project.

A negative NPV, however, does not necessarily mean that a project should be abandoned outright. What is indicated is that the project is not feasible in its present form. For example, if NPV analysis shows that a product line is not viable in light of the investment it requires, perhaps a higher price can be set, increasing cash inflows. Or perhaps changes in materials, design, or volume can bring down costs, again improving cash flow. Maybe the initial investment can be reduced by purchasing used machinery or by making use of currently excess capacity.

THE PRESENT VALUE INDEX

The present value index provides a way of comparing proposed capital projects to each other in terms of present value. It can be calculated as follows:

$$\text{Present value index} = \frac{\text{Total present value of cash inflow}}{\text{Initial investment}}$$

For example, the present value index of the screw machine project at the 15 percent hurdle rate is:

$$\frac{\$25{,}095}{\$20{,}000} = 1.25$$

If another project involves an initial investment of $35,000 and the present value of its resulting cash inflows at a 15 percent hurdle rate is $38,145, its present value index is 1.09. Since a higher present value index indicates a better cash return, a comparison of these two projects would weigh in favor of the screw machine.

INTERNAL RATE OF RETURN

The internal rate of return (IRR) is closely related to present value analysis. The NPV assumes a target or hurdle rate below which the cash flow from a project is inadequate to justify an investment. The IRR approach, however, seeks to determine the rate which makes the present value of the expected cash flows equal to the initial outlay of cash.

For example, in the NPV analysis of the screw machine project, the present value of cash flows, when discounted at 15 percent, exceeded the initial investment. At what rate of discounting would they equal the investment, that is, produce a NPV of zero? The answer is found by trial and error. Determine the present value of the cash flow when discounted at 20 percent and at 22 percent as shown in Exhibit 43. The IRR is between the two figures. Next, interpolate by multiplying the difference between the two discount rates (2%) by the difference between the two present values ($1,345) divided by the amount by which the higher present value exceeds the original investment ($965). Add the result to the lower discount rate (20%).

$$IRR = 20\% + \left(2\% \times \frac{\$\ 965}{\$1,345}\right) = 20\% + 1.4\% = 21.4\%$$

If the cash flows from the project are discounted at 21.4 percent, they will equal the initial investment. Rondack managers can now take this figure and compare it with the cost of capital, with the rate of return on alternative investments, or with the company's goals for return on capital. Where the NPV method only accepts or rejects a project based on its projected cash flows, the IRR method gives a figure for broad comparisons.

The trial and error method of calculating IRR can be cumbersome, particularly when you are dealing with a number of projects with complicated cash flows. Today, electronic calculators and small computers can readily perform the calculations and save you a great deal of time.

CALCULATING THE INTERNAL RATE OF RETURN
FOR RONDACK'S SCREW MACHINE

Year	Present Value Factor @ 20%	Actual Cash Inflow	Present Value of Cash Inflow
1	.833	$5,000	$ 4,165
2	.694	5,000	3,470
3	.579	5,000	2,895
4	.482	5,000	2,410
5	.402	5,000	2,010
6	.335	5,000	1,675
7	.279	5,000	1,395
8	.233	5,000	1,165
9	.194	5,000	970
10	.162	5,000	810
	Total present value		$20,965

Year	Present Value Factor @ 22%	Actual Cash Inflow	Present Value of Cash Inflow
1	.820	$5,000	$ 4,100
2	.672	5,000	3,360
3	.551	5,000	2,755
4	.451	5,000	2,255
5	.370	5,000	1,850
6	.303	5,000	1,515
7	.249	5,000	1,245
8	.204	5,000	1,020
9	.167	5,000	835
10	.137	5,000	685
	Total present value		$19,620

$$IRR = 20\% + (22\% - 20\%) \times \left(\frac{20,095 - 20,000}{20,095 - 19,620}\right)$$

$$IRR = 20\% + \left(2\% \times \frac{965}{1,345}\right)$$

$$IRR = 20\% + (2\% \times .71)$$

$$IRR = 20\% + 1.4\% = 21.4\%$$

Exhibit 43.
Calculating internal rate of return (IRR)

> **CASH FLOW ALERT—COMPUTER DEPARTMENT**
>
> Some nonfinancial managers are discouraged from getting involved in capital spending proposals because they are wary of the complex cash flow analysis required. Can you develop and make available to all managers simple, user-friendly software which guides them through the cash flow aspects of a project? A fill-in-the-blanks type of spreadsheet would be ideal.

RISK IN CAPITAL PROJECTS

By definition, a capital project means spending money today with the hope of receiving cash flow benefits in the future. But what if the cash flow does not materialize? A host of factors can affect the course of a project, either by raising costs or reducing benefits. Alternatively, a project can produce greater cash flow than anticipated.

How does the manager who is concerned about the rate of cash flow, perhaps because his company is experiencing a shortage of operating capital, deal with this risk factor? Several approaches are possible for rationalizing risk:

Cash Flow Range

This method involves making as accurate an estimate as possible of the potential levels of cash flow under the best and worst circumstances. For example, the manager who proposed the Rondack screw machine project might look at the fluctuation in the price of purchased screws, the cost of screw stock, the reliability of the machine, variations in maintenance costs, and other factors. He may then estimate that the annual cash flow advantage of the machine could range from $4,000 to $6,000 each year of its ten-year life. Present value analysis shows that at $4,000 annual cash flow the project would have a present value of $20,076 (discounted at the same 15 percent). At $6,000, the present value would be $30,114. Since both of these figures exceed the initial cost of $20,000, they indicate that the project is very low in risk.

But what if the calculations had determined that the cash inflows could be as low as $1,000 annually or as high as $8,000? The present value of the project in this case could drop to $5,019 or be as high as $40,152. The first figure indicates a negative net present value of $14,981. The second points to a large potential profit. Rondack managers would have to decide whether the company was ready to take the risk in light of this uncertainty. Among other factors, the company's cash position, its credit standing, and the importance of dependable future cash flows would have to be considered. But at least the cash flow range method takes some of the guesswork out of decision making and gives managers definite figures to work with.

CASH FLOW ALERT—ACCOUNTING DEPARTMENT

Estimates of future operating costs are essential to all forms of cash flow analysis. While engineering studies and the data of equipment manufacturers can supply some information, the core of these estimates is your company's own experience. Accurate and accessible cost accounting records are a valuable resource for making predictions. Make sure data is kept up-to-date and is available in convenient form to managers who are analyzing potential capital spending projects. If you can analyze specific trends in labor or maintenance costs, materials prices, or productivity, these can facilitate extrapolations.

Risk-adjusted Discounting

The riskier an investment, the higher the rate of return the investor looks for. In risk-adjusted discounting, a company's managers incorporate a risk factor into the discounting rate rather than basing it merely on the cost of capital. For example, the Rondack supervisor discounts the cash flows from the proposed screw machine at 15 percent. Assuming this represents the rate of return the company seeks on low-risk investments of this type, what if the project were judged to have a medium or high risk? Managers might then be required to discount cash flows at a higher rate. Maybe medium-risk ventures would have to pass a hurdle rate of 20 percent, high-risk projects a hurdle rate of 25 percent. The company would therefore purchase the machine if the risk associated with the projected cash flows were low or medium.

Determining into which category of risk a project fits requires judgment. You have to sit down and look at all the factors that could affect cash flow. You also have to compare the project to others in the various categories. A particular type of project may automatically fall into a certain classification. For example, fuel-saving projects may generally be considered low-risk, while a new product line will usually be seen as high-risk.

Sensitivity Analysis

This approach divides risk into separate components and weighs the changes in each component on the cash flow from the project. Its purpose is to identify those factors which are most important—that is, where a small change will have a significant impact on present value—so that they can be studied more closely.

A simple illustration can be derived from the Rondack screw machine example. The supervisor calculates the effect of a 10 percent increase in the initial cash outlay, resulting perhaps from installation costs for special wiring. He finds that this reduces NPV from $5,095 to $3,095, a 39 percent decrease. Next, he calculates the effect if, for some reason, annual cash flows were to be 10 percent lower than projected. In this situation, he finds that net present value drops by 49 percent. These figures indicate that the project is more sensitive to changes in cash flow than it is to changes in the initial cash outlay.

Sensitivity analysis becomes more important when dealing with complex projects. If your company is contemplating a major investment to bring a new product to market, calculate the effect of changes in such factors as price, sales volume, and key materials costs. You then can identify the most crucial risk factors involved. You may derive a table such as this:

Risk Factor	% Change in Factor	% Change in NPV
Initial investment	+10	−22
Basic material cost	+10	−36
Price	−10	−68
Sales volume	−10	−14

The table directs your attention first to selling price as a key risk factor. You will want to double-check things like past price fluctuations for similar products, current and potential competition, your sales force's estimates of a sustainable price, etc. Next you might want to check the stability of the cost of your basic material, perhaps lock in a long-term contract in order to reduce risk in this area as well. Initial investment level and sales volume, while important, are shown to be lower-priority risk factors.

CASH FLOW ALERT

The various methods of analysis discussed in this chapter are most commonly used to evaluate capital spending. However, their use is not limited. They can be employed to quantify the impact of any project intended to generate cash flow. These include advertising campaigns, research and development projects, modernization, product line or subsidiary acquisition, maintenance projects, computer software development, and so on. Focusing on cash flow is the best way to determine whether the proposed project is feasible.

IDENTIFYING CAPITAL PROJECTS

Payback period, net present value, IRR, and the other forms of analysis are all important ways to quantify the effect that capital spending will have on cash flow. But before you can analyze a project you have to identify one. Every manager, from shop foreman on up, should be on the lookout for ways to enhance cash flow.

Get into the habit of examining the various facets of your business regularly and asking, "How can cash flow be improved through spending in this area?" Here are some facets to consider:

Market. What products can be added to the company's line which, because of their relation to current products, could be introduced with minimal sales and marketing expense and high customer acceptance? Can an investment in a new product be "leveraged" by making use of currently idle plant capacity? Any method for holding down development and introduction costs and speeding up cash flows is likely to make a project more feasible.

Scrap. One company invested in a machine to separate three different types of metals from its combined scrap. The metals were sold to a recycling company. The resulting cash flow paid for the machine in three years and added to the company's cash coffers for another seven. A large hotel spent money on a trash compactor. Its cash flow was increased because of lower carting costs and less need for storage space. This cash flow repaid the price of the compactor in two years.

Fuel. Can the price of converting to another form of fuel be recouped quickly through lower fuel bills? Will an initial expenditure on a fuel-efficient machine pay for itself in fuel savings over the life of the machine?

Materials. One company found that an investment in a machine to work stainless steel paid off because it eliminated the need to plate certain parts. The cash flow from the reduced plating costs justified the investment. Could cheaper, more durable, materials, or ones that generate less scrap help to improve your cash flow?

Machinery. Numerically controlled and computer-controlled machines often justify their cost because they cut labor costs and thus increase cash flow. Can you spot examples of where automation can increase productivity or replace labor? The factory floor is not the only place where machinery can have an impact. For example, automated warehouses can enhance cash flows both by minimizing labor costs and maximizing utilization of space.

Procedures. How can your company improve cash flow by operating differently? For example, one company invested in equipment to use formerly waste heat from refractory ovens to heat its offices and engineering building in the winter. Lower fuel bills increased cash flow. Another company saved on labor costs by delivering parts to work stations by means of an overhead conveyor system.

CASH FLOW ALERT—PRODUCTION

Many companies put a low priority on maintenance investment. Machines or facilities are used until an urgent problem develops, then emergency measures are taken. Maintenance operations may be completed, but spending on replacement, upgrading, or overhaul of equipment is put off. Production managers should make an effort to alert their supervisors to the need for prudent investment in maintenance. Use cash flow analysis to show how money spent today can pay off in reduced costs down the road. Watch out for worthwhile opportunities in these areas.

EVALUATING CAPITAL PROJECTS

All capital spending must be evaluated in terms of cash flow. A new product line, for example, may yield large profits three or four years after introduction. But if initial investment required is large, and the early cash flows are minimal, then the project, however profitable, may not be within the capacity of a company with limited cash and credit resources. Or the firm may not be willing to risk what financial resources are available.

Priorities are also important. Every company's cash resources are limited. Given the choice between potentially profitable projects, how are managers to choose one over another? Again, cash flow is often the deciding factor. A short payback period and attractive net present value weigh heavily in favor of a project. Depending on the company's cash position, its managers may be looking primarily for projects with low initial cost, with substantial early cash flows, or with a high long-term rate of return.

In order to give financial managers a basis for choosing capital projects, operating managers throughout the company should prepare uniform capital spending proposals which give as detailed a picture as possible of the cash flow implications of any capital spending. Exhibit 44 illustrates such a proposal. Exhibit 45 is a blank form that you can reproduce to use in your company.

This formal evaluation provides several advantages. First, it gives individual managers a way to evaluate "blue sky" ideas. Often, a project seems attractive at first but does not prove to yield sufficient cash flows on closer examination. Second, it forces managers to commit themselves to concrete figures on estimated costs and cash flows, giving decision makers a solid view of the merits of a project. And finally, it facilitates the comparison of different projects and provides a basis for setting spending priorities.

Of course, it must be recognized that the results always depend on the accuracy of the cash flow projections. For this reason, the narrative description of risk factors is important. Managers can often become overly optimistic about pet projects. A sober consideration of the risks involved is essential to a good evaluation and decision.

CREATIVE APPROACHES TO CAPITAL SPENDING

Once the close connection between capital spending and cash flow is grasped, the manager should always be alert to ways to enhance the cash flow from proposed spending projects. This doesn't mean minimizing spending, but getting the healthiest overall cash flow from every dollar spent. Below are a few ideas to stimulate thinking in this area:

- Used equipment—from punch presses to computers—can often substantially lower initial investment in a project without reducing cash flow.
- Joint ventures may be feasible for companies lacking the cash resources to enter into projects alone.

- Unused capacity—whether of a machine, a vehicle, or office space—always represents an opportunity. How can it be put to use to generate cash? For example, can a warehouse be rented out until it is needed?

CASH FLOW ALERT—PRODUCTION

Look for inventory bottlenecks. Work-in-progress inventory can be reduced if materials and products flow smoothly from beginning to end of the production process. For example, one company found that parts were always piling up at the plating department. The addition of another plating machine and improved scheduling in that sector reduced WIP stocks by 20 percent.

CAPITAL SPENDING EVALUATION FORM

Submitted by J. Jones   Date November 12, 19—

Department Assembly   Title supervisor

Project name Screw machine

Project description Install machine to make numbers 5, 6, 7, 12 and 14 screws, currently purchased

Source of cash flow enhancement (e.g., cost reduction, revenue increase, etc.) cost reduction

Period (mo./qtr./yr.)	Direct Cash Benefit	Depreciation	Tax Benefit @ 40% Rate	Total Cash Benefit	Present Value Factor (@ 15%)	Present Value
1	$4,200	$2,000	$800	$5,000	.870	$ 4,350
2	4,200	2,000	800	5,000	.756	3,780
3	4,200	2,000	800	5,000	.658	3,290
4	4,200	2,000	800	5,000	.572	2,860
5	4,200	2,000	800	5,000	.497	2,485
6	4,200	2,000	800	5,000	.432	2,160
7	4,200	2,000	800	5,000	.376	1,880
8	4,200	2,000	800	5,000	.327	1,635
9	4,200	2,000	800	5,000	.248	1,420
10	4,200	2,000	800	5,000	.247	1,235

Total present value $25,095

Present value index 1.25   Initial cost   20,000

Payback period 4 years   Net present value $ 5,095

Risk category (high/medium/low)   low

Risk factors Price of screw stock has fluctuated by 15% past 5 years.

Exhibit 44.
Example of capital spending evaluation form

CAPITAL SPENDING EVALUATION FORM

Submitted by _____ Date _____

Department _____ Title _____

Project name _____

Project description _____

_____

Source of cash flow enhancement (e.g., cost reduction, revenue increase, etc.) _____

Period (mo./qtr./year)	Direct Cash Benefit	Depreciation	Tax Benefit @ 40% Rate	Total Cash Benefit	Present Value Factor (@ %)	Present Value
1						
2						
3						
4						
5						
6						
7						
8						
9						
10						

Total present value _____

Present value index _____ Initial cost _____

Payback period _____ Net present value _____

Risk category (high/medium/low) _____

Risk factors _____

_____

Exhibit 45.
Blank form of capital spending evaluation

11

IMPROVING CASH FLOW IN THE PRODUCTION PROCESS

Some of the most fruitful areas for speeding the inflow of cash and slowing its outflow can be found in your production facilities. Most production costs, especially for labor and materials, strain cash flow because of their size. All delays and disruptions of production do the same by slowing down cash receipts.

Begin exploring opportunities to improve cash flow by asking yourself the following questions about your production activities. Then go on and review the proven techniques in the remainder of this chapter for squeezing cash out of your manufacturing process.

- Are labor costs carefully tracked and held to a minimum?
- Is overtime avoided whenever possible?
- Do we constantly look for ways to improve labor productivity?
- Do our machinery and equipment work at maximum capacity most of the time?
- Could machines that are idle be put to use or sold?
- Do we have extra space—warehouse, branch offices, etc.—which is underutilized and could be used, sold, or rented?
- Have we identified all sources of production delays and taken efforts to reduce them?

- Are customer orders filled as quickly and accurately as possible?
- Where is cash being wasted? On scrap? Inefficient energy use? Excess paperwork?

REVIEWING SETUP SCHEDULES

Setup times and schedules, plus the length of production runs, can play an important part in determining your company's cash flow. To begin with, make sure that you take into account ease of setup when investing in machinery. One of the advantages that Japanese companies have over U.S. firms is that their machinery is designed for quick changeover of tools. This not only trims downtime, but also allows shorter production runs, lower inventory levels, greater flexibility, and generally reduced costs.

CASH FLOW ALERT

Be sure to consolidate the need for common parts from all areas of the company into one schedule in order to avoid unneeded repetition of setup and frequent abbreviated runs.

Even with your current machinery, however, you should analyze carefully the cash flow implications of production runs. The Avenal Co. is a maker of industrial pumps. The firm's engineers estimated the cost of setting up an automatic welding machine at $1,200 per run. Because of this cost, the company was producing components on the machine in monthly runs. This meant, though, that they had to maintain a higher average inventory of the item. One manager decided to compare the current costs to those that would be incurred if Avenal switched to weekly runs. Exhibit 46 shows what he found.

The manager discovered that in spite of the higher setup costs, a weekly production run would actually improve the company's annual cash flow by $47,172. In addition, there would be a onetime im-

IMPROVING CASH FLOW IN THE PRODUCTION PROCESS 153

	Monthly Runs	Weekly Runs
Cost of setup per run	$ 1,200	$ 1,200
Setups per year	12	52
Yearly setup cost	$ 14,400	$ 62,400
Annual production	100,000	100,000
Lot size (units)	8,333	1,923
Average inventory	4,167	966
Safety stocks	1,500	375
Total average inventory	5,667	1,341
Cost per unit	$100	$100
Average inventory value	$566,700	$134,100
Inventory carrying cost (@ 22%)	124,674	29,502
Total cost	$139,074	$ 91,902
Inventory reduction cash flow	—	$432,600

Exhibit 46.
Cash flow of monthly and weekly production runs

provement of $432,600 as a result of reducing the average investment in inventory. You can perform similar analyses on your own machinery in order to find optimum production runs.

PRODUCTION EFFICIENCY

Production efficiency is a key, and often overlooked, element in the cash flow equation. It can influence everything from inventory levels, to labor costs, to speed of order filling. An efficient manufacturing facility always enhances a company's cash flow.

Naturally, many cash flow improvement techniques will be unique to your business. The important thing is for all managers to be constantly on the lookout for creative ways to speed up the inflow of cash through changes in production procedures and methods. The following is a list of typical production efficiencies that companies have introduced for the sake of better cash flow from operations:

- Don't keep production workers waiting for parts. This is one of the most common ways of wasting labor and adding to costs.
- Never move parts more than necessary. Better to have a forklift truck deposit a pallet of parts at a work station than to move them to an intermediate area and require workers to keep replenishing their supplies.
- Eliminate clutter. Not only does clutter—tools, equipment, benches, excess parts—hamper production efficiency, but it often represents excess inventory that should be classified, used, or scrapped to generate cash.
- Cut order picking time by clearly labeling and arranging bins and storage areas. A delay in shipping means a delay in cash receipts.
- Eliminate all hand movement of materials if possible. Such approaches as an overhead conveyor system can easily repay their costs and contribute to cash flow through lower labor expenses for many years.
- Automate. Don't overlook any area where automation can contribute to lower costs. Always ask if automation can:
    -Reduce scrap,
    -Replace labor,
    -Improve quality.
Consider not only the automation of actual work, but automatic tool changes and material movement. Card readers to open doors can introduce automation to the security function, word processors can bring it to clerical work.
- Standardize. Never pass up an opportunity to standardize: Can a production worker increase his output if he can use fewer standard tools? Where can standard parts cut inventory and assembly costs? Will standard lubricants, solvents, and cleaning materials allow both bulk purchases and work simplification? Can minor design alterations allow the use of standard parts in products, eliminating the need for expensive custom parts? Will inter-

CASH FLOW ALERT

Bring your engineering department into the cash flow improvement program by having them:

Check cost trends in the use of machinery and materials

Be aware of specific high-cost areas during product design

Compare actual with estimated labor costs

Review part obsolescence and standardization

Analyze feedback on customer preferences from marketing managers during design projects

Standardize—that should be the watchword of engineering when it comes to contributing to inventory management. For example, one manufacturer of compressors used five different sizes of bolts in the housing of one of its products depending on the amount of stress each had to withstand. But a study uncovered the fact that if the strongest bolt were used in all five applications, inventories of the items could be cut by two-thirds. The savings from improved cash flow more than made up for the marginally higher cost of the heavier bolts. Where can you standardize?

How can modifying the form of the product help cut inventory? For example, one company which produces rubber tubing stopped stocking various lengths and simply kept long rolls of each size to be cut to the customer's orders. An auto replacement parts company made connecting hoses with either right- or left-handed brackets attached. The firm found that they could cut inventories of the item almost in half by including both brackets with a single hose. The customer discarded the one not used. The slightly higher production cost was more than outweighed by the savings through standardization.

changeability between products or models allow longer production runs and other efficiencies? Are part numbers and classifications standardized?
- Labor economy. "Do it right the first time" is a slogan that you should constantly emphasize to workers. Make sure they know that they're at work to produce, not just to put in their time. Track overtime costs by department to spot problem areas. More important, look into the reasons for even "normal" overtime.

CASH FLOW ALERT

Do you have a system to check the current status of any job? Are records kept for each machine to allow you to track downtime, repairs, and other delays that will affect production scheduling?

The copy of your purchase order that accompanies the shipment of goods should not include the amount ordered. This forces the receiving clerk to accurately count and record the amount delivered. It discourages excess or deficient shipments and enhances receiving-dock security.

Many companies tie up assets in stocking inventory to service slow-moving or out-of-production lines. Ordering parts as needed or making them to order can often cut inventories and improve cash flow. Consider the alternatives before making a commitment to a large inventory of service parts.

- Plant layout. Sometimes as a manufacturing facility grows, the design becomes haphazard and inefficient. Are inventory storage areas, tool cribs, work areas, machinery, etc., located in the most efficient relationship to each other? Can alterations in plant layout speed the flow of production? Is space being used as efficiently as possible?

- Ensure plant safety. Insisting on proper safety equipment and procedures costs the company little. Delays and higher insurance premiums resulting from accidents cut immediately into cash flow.
- Control materials. Make sure you account for all materials, components, and tools. If all materials are not either used, scrapped, or returned to stock, find out why. Use a system of vouchers when issuing standard parts.

CASH FLOW ALERT

Requiring skilled workers and craftsmen to own the standard tools used on the job improves cash flow by cutting company investment, encouraging careful use, and eliminating pilfering.

The Japanese have pioneered the Just-in-Time (JIT) method of production scheduling, in which materials and components are delivered just before they are needed in production. They are moved from the loading docks directly to the production floor. Supplier schedules and shipping arrangements may keep this approach from being feasible for your company, but it's a goal to shoot for. Would small lots of expensive inventory items, delivered on a tight schedule, help you to cut inventory investment? The U.S. auto industry has picked up on the idea, reconsidering once typical rail carload purchases. General Motors recently cut inventories of parts and raw materials by 20 percent in three years despite increasing production by a third.

EXPLORING PRODUCTION SCHEDULING

Parts are not received from a vendor on time, so a production line must be shut down. A large customer order is lost because stocks are not on hand when they are needed. Machines sit idle waiting for operators. Operators sit idle waiting for parts. All of these are symptoms of poor production scheduling. Some of the most severe cash flow problems can be traced back to this source. The only solution is endless management diligence and attention to detail. Put special emphasis on:

Forecasting and planning. Production managers should always look ahead. What level of sales is projected? How long are vendor lead times likely to be? What rate of production can be expected from a machine or worker? Are backup machines likely to be needed? Are they available? When will a machine need to be shut down for maintenance? For how long? Anticipate all of these factors and work out a schedule that meets production requirements.

Communication. Production control managers should be kept aware at all times of any order changes. Has a major new order arrived? Did an important customer cancel an order? Is a new product selling well?

But communication should not be limited to actual sales. Production people should know about significant marketing plans or promotions that are likely to generate sales in the future. They should be in touch with purchasing managers to keep up on vendor lead times and potential supply shortages. The more information production planners have, the more accurately and efficiently they can plan.

CASH FLOW ALERT

Poll the sales force regularly. What do they expect to sell in coming months? They have the best view of current and potential sales levels. Communicate changes anticipated, trends, and projections to all concerned.

Eliminating bottlenecks. Just as a chain is only as strong as its weakest link, so production processes cannot move faster than their slowest step. Trace the flow of production in your facility and identify bottlenecks. These need not be actual production operations, but could be transportation links such as movements from one building to another. Or they could involve inspection or record-keeping steps. Look, too, for areas that could develop into bottlenecks if production needed to be stepped up to meet a surge in demand.

Keeping records. Efficient production scheduling can only derive from accurate records. Actual rates of work for machines and manpower must be charted. The reasons for idleness must be tracked before idleness can be reduced. Detailed records help set realistic work standards and contribute to the reliability of forecasts.

SCRAP AND CASH FLOW

Scrap always has a direct effect on cash flow. It literally means money down the drain. While no manufacturer can eliminate all scrap, control of scrap must play a part in your cash flow improvement program. Here are five points you should always pay attention to:

1. Track production efficiency. How much scrap and rework is generated for each unit sold? Are trends positive or negative? What is the reason for an increase in scrap? If you don't keep records and monitor them carefully, you won't be able to answer these questions.

2. Pinpoint trouble spots. Is a particular machine, department, or shift contributing excess scrap? One company traced a large production of its scrap problems to workers' careless feeding of machines. Guide bars that prevented the practice reduced scrap costs by 20 percent. You will often find that a few operations are the biggest contributors to scrap and the most fruitful areas for action.

CASH FLOW ALERT

Always separate avoidable scrap (e.g., poorly assembled products) from necessary scrap (such as wastage from a machine). Compare levels to industry averages and look for ways to improve on avoidable scrap output.

---

3. Don't waste money on scrap. A manager at a company that manufactured plumbing fixtures found that scrap pipe, while waiting to be sold to a recycling company, was being stored in a heated warehouse. Piling it outside instead improved warehouse utilization and efficiency. Do you spend money moving scrap from one place to another? Does it have to be sorted, rather than being separated at its place of origin?

4. Work with vendors. How can the materials and components that are shipped to you be designed to cut scrap levels? Are you insisting on top-quality goods? Do you have any provisions to recover the cost of inferior materials from the vendor? Will a different specification of materials result in less scrap?

5. Avoid scrapping finished goods. Rework is often a better solution to defective finished goods. Remember that when you scrap products or components you are scrapping not just the materials but also the value of the labor and overhead that they have already absorbed.

QUALITY CONTROL

Poor quality, whether it results in production inefficiencies, scrapped materials and products, or customer dissatisfaction, always has a negative impact on cash flow. Begin your quality control effort not with inspection or testing, but with purchasing. Make sure you are buying the proper quality of materials and components and that you are getting what you pay for.

Routine examination of incoming supplies should become a habit in every company. Afterward, a wide-ranging in-house quality program that emphasizes every detail from assembly to packaging should be applied. With the right approach, high-quality costs little but contributes substantially to cash flow. Quality control experts recommend that every program include four fundamental elements:

Specifications. They should be applied at every stage of the production process. Vendors should know what they are and realize that you will insist on them. The same goes for your own foremen and department heads. Don't rely on vague terms like "high quality." Make it specific: tensile strength, tolerances, fail rate, etc.

Prevention. Quality control should emphasize operations that prevent defects, not inspections that detect them. Naturally, you will require inspection and testing, but these functions should always feed back directly into the production process with the idea of preventing quality defects. For example, one company conducted an in-depth study of quality control problems and found that worker error was behind many diverse defects. Stepped-up training improved quality by 45 percent.

Perfection. All quality programs should be targeted at zero defects, not for some "acceptable" level of failure that may breed complacency. While perfection will never be attained, it should always be aimed at because it forces all employees to continue to strive for higher and higher quality.

Cost. Always evaluate quality in terms of expense. How much does it add to unit costs when a certain percent of goods has to be scrapped? What is the cost of downtime when shoddy materials jam a machine? What is the cost of reworking finished products? This not only highlights the seriousness of quality problems, but guides managers toward economical methods for eliminating them.

CASH FLOW ALERT

Take your suggestion program seriously. Your workers are often the best source of ideas for improving quality and enhancing manufacturing efficiency. Determine the validity of each suggestion and give out awards based on savings realized.

Reliability is an often overlooked factor in inventory management. If you experience a 10 percent rejection rate on a vendor's parts, then your inventory of that part will have to be at least 10 percent higher. If delivery schedules are erratic, larger safety stocks will be needed. Insisting on quality and prompt delivery can help

> keep inventory down. The General Electric Co. uses an incentive system called the Vendor 100 Club to reward suppliers for consistent quality. Can you start a similar program at your company? As quality and reliability improve, trim inventories accordingly.

CONSERVATION

The American Can Co. substituted ultraviolet light for heat when curing the coatings on cans. The outcome: less energy use, lower capital costs, less scrap, and shorter runs. All of these benefited the company's cash flow.

The Carborundum Co. set up an elaborate but inexpensive system to track exactly where its energy dollars were being spent. This enabled it to plug wasteful energy usage, to track the effects of conservation measures, and to reduce energy costs to a minimum.

Conservation represents a fruitful area for improving cash flow. For example, up to 95 percent of the energy consumed by an incandescent light bulb is given off as heat. If your facility is air conditioned, you are not only wasting energy, but paying to remove the waste product. Fluorescent fixtures may significantly cut costs.

Other conservation ideas range from proper maintenance of boilers, to storm windows, insulation, and recycling of energy used in processing. For most companies, energy costs are an ongoing and significant drain on cash flow. Abrupt increases in prices, as have become common in recent decades, can severely restrict cash flow in vulnerable companies.

SHIPPING

This is another frequently overlooked area for cash flow improvement. Not only do shipping costs make your company's products more expensive, but products damaged during shipping represent a serious quality control problem. Look for creative ways to make shipping both cheaper and safer.

For example, the Westinghouse Electric Corp. glues together appliance containers during shipping to create a unified load. This eliminates much of the damage from vibration. Some die casters have had suppliers deliver raw aluminum in molten form rather than as ingots. While adding somewhat to shipping costs, this drastically reduces the casters' cost of reheating the material. Another company was able to cut shipping costs 30 percent simply by redesigning packages so that more could be fit onto trucks.

CASH FLOW ALERT

The receiving manager should be aware too that he can serve as an early warning point for inventory problems. Has a supplier changed his delivery procedure so that goods are arriving sooner or later than previously? Are suppliers shipping more than the amount of goods ordered? Could a supplier switch to a different mode of transportation—a small van, a full rail car—in order to save both you and himself money? Are parts being damaged because of poor shipping procedures or inadequate packaging? Receiving is your first line of defense against the cash flow drain of excess and obsolete inventory.

VALUE ANALYSIS

This approach has been used by many companies to realize significant cash flow improvements. Value analysis (VA) might be defined as cost cutting in depth. While traditional cost cutting programs ask "*How* can we do it more cheaply?" value analysis programs ask "*Why* do we do it at all?" Can the product be redesigned to cut manufacturing costs? Can different, less expensive materials or more standard parts be used?

A value analysis program should result in a systematic rethinking of every aspect of both materials and production. VA teams consisting of engineers, production managers, assembly workers, purchasers, and quality personnel should look at these areas with two ideas in mind: function and value. What is the purpose of a product component or processing step? How can the same value be achieved at lower cost?

For example, one company was mounting an assembly onto a motor with four standard hex screws, each using two washers. Value analysis resulted in a change to a screw with a built-in washer. Not only did this screw cost less than the combined screws and washers, but it provided a better-quality mounting with lower assembly costs. A small change, but multiplied over the scope of the manufacturing process, a lucrative one.

CASH FLOW ALERT

Target cost-cutting efforts by examining a product's components. For example, the cost of an electric clock might be broken down to:

Electrical components	55% of cost
Works	26% " "
Casing	11% " "
Manufacturing	8% " "

Therefore, a cost reduction of 10 percent applied to the manufacturing process would cut total costs only .8 percent. The same reduction applied to the electrical components, however, would reduce costs by 5.5 percent. The magnitude of cash flow improvement in each case becomes clearer.

MAKE OR BUY?

Making a component, rather than purchasing it from an outside vendor, can have important cash flow implications. Maybe you can produce the part more cheaply. Inventory can be held at lower levels because you control the source of supply. Quality standards can be

Cost to buy (per unit)	$5.50	
Usage per year	100,000	
Total yearly cost		$550,000
Cost to make (per year):		
Materials	$185,000	
Labor	120,000	
Variable overhead	57,000	
Increased fixed overhead	62,000	
Increased administrative cost	14,000	
Reduction in inventory carrying cost*	(7,040)	
Total		$431,040
Usage per year	100,000	
Unit cost	$4.31	
Total savings to make		$118,960

Note: Average inventory reduced by $32,000 @ 22% carrying charge.

Exhibit 47.
Calculating the make/buy decision

improved. And the dependence on suppliers can be eliminated, avoiding shortages, late deliveries, and price increases. All of these factors will improve cash flow.

In some cases, substantial investment in equipment or facilities will be necessary in order to make the part. If this is true, then the decision becomes one of justifying the capital spending according to the methods described elsewhere in this book.

But often a part can be produced with minimal additional investment. In that case, the decision will turn on a quantitative comparison of the cost of making the part with the cost of purchasing it. For example, the Birch Corp. was purchasing the metal housing that it used in the electrical components it sold. While it had a good relationship with the supplier, the firm's managers wondered whether it would be advisable to make the housings themselves. They currently paid $5.50 for each piece and used 100,000 pieces a year. Their analysis of the options is shown in Exhibit 47.

The calculation indicates that it would be cheaper to make the item than to purchase it. Birch's cash flow would increase by a solid $118,960 each year.

CASH FLOW ALERT

Cash flow disruptions can result from materials shortages. What can you do to lock in supplies of potentially scarce goods? For example, the Cabot Corp., faced with possible shortages of chromium and other metals, introduced strategies such as buying ores in the ground and entering joint ventures with refiners.

Always get full details on requisitions. For example, the production department asks for an order of a particular model of air wrench. Purchasing managers should find out the actual torque needed and then ask the supplier for the least expensive model that will fill the need, instead of accepting the requisition at face value.

Improved communications offer purchasing innovations. For example, a General Electric Co. division cut inventories by $200,000 by computerizing communications with one supplier. Buyers can place an order by 11 a.m. and receive delivery the same day.

12

IMPROVING OPERATIONS AND PROCEDURES TO CONSERVE CASH

There are usually thousands of opportunities in every firm to enhance cash flow by improving operations and procedures. All that is needed is for all managers—from the machine shop foreman to office manager to controller to chief engineer—to begin thinking in terms of cash flow. How to speed the inflow of cash, how to slow its outflow, and how to use it more effectively.

ACCOUNTING

Accurate, detailed cost accounting is an essential tool for spotting and plugging cash flow leaks. One firm, for example, reviewed its allocation of variable overhead expenses and found that a product previously thought profitable actually represented a substantial drain on cash flow. The product was discontinued, and the cash position improved.

Accounting employees should go beyond mere financial record keeping. For example, accountants should verify the justification for a machine purchase or other capital spending. They should then follow up to make sure that the cash flow predictions prove to be true in practice and that future decisions take advantage of this experience. They should make detailed analyses of labor, materials, and overhead costs, tracking trends and comparing them to industry averages. They should spot high-cost problems with particular projects or product lines and make efforts to identify the cash flow drains involved.

It is important that a company's accountants and financial managers develop a cash sense. Too often, accountants look merely at the profit shown by accrual accounting. They don't take into account the timing of cash flows, the working capital investment required by operational changes, or the limited availability or cost of cash.

SELLING COSTS

Selling costs usually represent a fruitful area for cash flow improvements. For example, sales commissions, in lieu of salary or part of salary, may provide additional motivation for effective selling. In addition, it has two direct cash flow benefits. First, it delays the expenditure of cash until after the sale is made. Second, it directly links selling costs with sales levels, which prevents a cash drain during a sales slump.

Direct sales costs are another area for cash flow improvements. How can your sales representatives make better use of the telephone in order to cut the cost of sales calls? The cost of sales calls is skyrocketing. Can the structure of the sales force be rearranged, or routes and territories changed, so as to save on costs and improve coverage? Would better training help to make sales efforts more effective?

CASH FLOW ALERT

Cut sales costs for slow-moving or marginal products by putting them into a catalog—your own or a distributor's—instead of selling them directly.

Make sure, too, that your salesmen do not indirectly hamper cash flows. Do they sell to customers who are unacceptable credit risks, or who frequently cancel orders? These tactics can result in excess inventory and bad debt levels. Do they give out too many discounts and price breaks? This can cut into margins and cash flow without adding sufficiently to volume.

LEGAL COSTS

In 1977, TRW Inc. was involved in a multimillion-dollar patent infringement case. Rather than face the long delays and hundreds of thousands of dollars in legal fees that are standard with such litigation, the company agreed with the opposing party to settle the dispute in a unique way. Top executives from both companies sat down in a room with a third-party mediator. The evidence was presented over a number of days and an agreement, acceptable to both sides, was reached in a half hour.

Alternative dispute resolution like this is an opportunity for all companies to hold down the legal expenses that represent a significant cash flow drain even for the winner of a suit. Professional arbitration, so-called "rent-a-judge" proceedings, and dispute mediation centers, all provide similar quick and less expensive alternatives.

Often, these methods provide a further benefit. While courts can usually only award monetary damages, disputants can agree through arbitration to restitution that does not require cash expenditures. For example, maybe your company can agree to replace a product or provide free service in a case involving a breech of warranty, rather than having to pay the complainant a certain amount of damages. Also, arbitration and mediation usually don't generate the ill-will that arises from litigation. They can save you a customer or supplier who might have been lost in the rancor of a lawsuit.

When you do become involved in litigation, remember the time value of cash. Suppose your company experiences damage from a structural fault in a building addition. You sue the contractor for $100,000. He agrees to pay you only $65,000. You know that going to court will involve at least a three-year delay before a final settlement. A quick present value analysis will show you that, at an 18 percent discount rate, even if you receive the entire $100,000 after three years, it will have a value today of only $60,900. You're clearly better off, from a cash flow perspective, to take the $65,000 rather than fight for the entire $100,000. The difficulty of collecting awards even after they are made by a court reinforces this approach.

GIVEAWAYS

One way to spot hidden cash flow improvement opportunities is to review your entire business and ask, "What do we give away?" At first, you might answer, "Nothing." But stop and consider:

- Do we pay for shipping, or does the customer?
- Are employees allowed to take home finished products? What are they worth?
- Do we give away free credit to customers who habitually pay late?
- Are we too willing to make alterations in productions to suit customers while charging nothing for the service?
- Do we accept returns without adding a service charge?
- Do we provide free engineering advice?

All giveaways have a direct impact on cash flow. Sometimes they can be justified by competitive conditions. Customers may turn to other suppliers, for example, if your company will not make next-day deliveries. Other times, giveaways are nothing more than long-standing customs. Airlines, for example, once made a practice of giving away meals on almost all flights. "No frills" flights proved that customers were not particularly attracted by the meals. Now, most airlines have reduced or eliminated these giveaways on shorter flights.

You might find the same thing is true with something as basic as trade credit. What if you reduced terms to 30 days instead of 60 days? Would you really lose business? Or would you merely reduce the level of receivables outstanding and thus improve cash flow? Are you offering the terms for competitive reasons, or only because they are customary in your industry?

One way to approach this area is to adopt the "no frills" concept yourself. Instead of automatically including shipping, or delivery, or service with your product, make them optional. Let customers pay a slightly lower base price for the product, and then offer the additional items for fees that will cover their costs.

AUDITS

Some auditing firms specialize in examining utility, telephone, insurance, and shipping bills in order to make sure no overpayments have been made. Because of the complicated tariff and rate schedules involved, mistakes are common in these areas. The auditors are experienced in spotting them. Not only can they produce substantial refunds on past overpayments—usually any amounts paid incorrectly during the past three years—but they can plug future cash drains as well by advising you on the rates you should be paying. Since these firms work primarily on a contingency basis, their services do not impose a direct cash charge on your company.

INSURANCE

Two cash flow effects of insurance are important to examine. First, insurance can protect cash flows, especially during vulnerable periods. For example, maybe your company is in a period of expansion, and sales growth has led to a tight cash situation. While bad debts are always serious, the default of an important customer at this point would be disastrous. The solution is to insure your receivables. For a small cost, your cash stream can be protected. The same holds for fidelity bonds. Insuring employees who have access to large amounts of funds protects you from disastrous losses you can't afford.

While insurance is decidedly useful, it also represents a cash flow drain. Many creative opportunities exist for cutting down on the cost of insurance. Large firms have moved increasingly to self-insurance, setting up pools of funds to cover routine claims and purchasing only enough insurance to protect against true catastrophes. Smaller companies can accomplish similar results by raising the deductible amount in their property and casualty insurance, assuming more risk but reducing premiums and thus improving cash flow.

An example was found in a company in the semiconductor industry. Many employees were young and single. As a result, claims against the company's medical insurance were low. Rather than pay relatively high insurance rates, the firm turned to self-insurance backed up by catastrophe protection. The cash savings amounted to $40,000 per year.

Another tactic is for smaller firms to form safety groups. For example, if ten companies who have a low history of casualty losses approach an insurer as a group and certify that they all take measures to keep claims down, they may well receive a substantial reduction in premiums.

CASH FLOW ALERT

You can adjust the timing of the cash flow burden of insurance premiums by negotiations with your insurance company. For example, you may be able to arrange to pay premiums that come due during your peak selling season later, after you've collected receipts from your customers.

EMPLOYEE RELATIONS

The most valuable of a company's assets, its people, is a valuable source of cash flow improvement. If an experienced worker leaves the company and has to be replaced, the cost of hiring and training the new employee, along with poorer performance as he or she progresses along the learning curve, can cost a company $5,000 or more.

Excessive turnover, then, is a serious and unnecessary drain on cash flow. How does your company's turnover rate compare with the average in your industry or geographic area? Is it increasing? Can it be improved? Are workers who leave the company for any reason routinely questioned to uncover the cause of their departure? Do you have specific programs to maintain the morale of hourly employees?

Supervision and training are vitally important factors in this area. One firm improved cash flow by an estimated $45,000 each month simply by putting all first-line supervisors through a seminar in effective communication. Making sure that lines of authority are clear can also help. Review your organization chart to make sure it's up-to-date and practical. Goal-oriented job descriptions are equally useful in making sure that the cash invested in employment produces the desired results.

Health care costs are another area where companies can experience a cash drain. Alarmed by skyrocketing medical costs, many companies have begun to introduce cost-containment programs. For example, rather than provide a full range of health benefits for every employee, companies offer a choice of plans and let the employees choose those they want up to a maximum cost. Rather than providing insurance that pays for 100 percent of benefits, more firms are requiring employees to contribute a portion of the cost. This not only reduces the company's direct costs, but lowers total costs by making employees reluctant to seek unnecessary treatment.

CASH FLOW ALERT

If your business is increasing and you want to save on labor costs, you might follow the example of some U.S. auto makers. Rather than hire new workers, they have invited retired workers to come back and work part- or full-time. This lowers cost by eliminating the expense of training and breaking in the employees. It also cuts benefit costs because the companies provide no additional pension or other benefits to these workers.

MAINTENANCE

Are your maintenance stocks excessive? In many companies they are. They may be less tightly controlled than ordinary inventories, but they represent the same burden on cash flow. You will find that because they are usually standard items like lubricants and spare parts, they can be held at lower levels without any adverse effect on operations.

Are routine maintenance operations monitored and scheduled just as thoroughly as production tasks, or are they carried out haphazardly or "as needed"? The latter can result in a lack of maintenance and in turn produce malfunctions or waste of labor.

When employees are assigned to repair work, they should, whenever possible, have standards and be adequately supervised. In addition, the reasons for equipment malfunctions should always be investigated and recorded, so that future breakdowns can be prevented.

COMMUNICATIONS

Communication expenses can eat into cash flows. To reduce them:

- Send letters instead of phoning. A large New York–based corporation found that more than a third of the telephone costs made by employees could have been more efficiently, and inexpensively, handled through the mail.
- Use a telex. This combines the speed of the telephone with the accuracy and lower cost of written communication.
- Look into lower-cost phone service. A private line between facilities in different cities may be less costly than long-distance calls.
- Reduce private use of telephone lines. Make sure that employees are familiar with company policy regarding private calls. Eliminate extra phones that are usually unsupervised.

CLERICAL COSTS

Usually, a company's clerical system grows in a much more haphazard way than the rest of its operations. Each department may develop its own record-keeping and filing system. Valuable space may be wasted by storing documents that are no longer needed. Here are a few tips for cutting down on clerical costs:

- Establish a central records office where all documents are stored. Make sure that it is well organized, accessible, and uses as many standard documents as possible.
- Purge files on a regular basis, at least annually. Code any of the previous year's documents to be retained and destroy the rest.
- Use microfilm and microfiche to both reduce the space needed for records and to preserve them in a more orderly fashion.
- Centralize typing and secretarial services for greater efficiency of use.
- Investigate the use of word processing equipment to cut down on routine typing.
- Make sure that documents do not have to be handled repeatedly.
- Control the use of copying machines to prevent overuse or unauthorized use. Centralized copying facilities may be more efficient and secure.

FORMS

You pay for all the forms you use in your business twice: once when you buy them and again when your employees spend time filling them out. Cash flow improvements begin when you review all forms and decide whether you need them at all. What purpose do they serve? Can they be combined into multiple-use forms? Next, look at the design. Is it arranged so that it can be filled in easily and accurately? Are forms routed in the most efficient way? Are purchase orders, invoices, etc., sequentially numbered and accounted for?

Errors are the most costly aspect of paperwork. Are your forms designed to minimize errors? For example, a large department store introduced a purchase order form which, when typed, produced five copies. One was retained by the purchasing department, three were sent to the supplier, and one was passed on to the buyer who'd requested the purchase. The supplier, in turn, retained one copy, returned one to purchasing to indicate any back order, and sent one on with the shipment. This last copy left out the quantity ordered, forcing the company's receiving clerks to verify the actual number received rather than assuming that it was the same as the number on the form. The introduction of this form reduced errors by 40 percent while cutting paperwork and delays. This, in turn, helped to improve cash flow.

ZERO-BASE BUDGETING

The marketing manager comes to a budget meeting and says that advertising expenditures should be increased next year by $20,000. His reason is that this year's budget was $200,000 and sales are expected to increase 10 percent in the coming year. Therefore, advertising expenditures should grow by a similar amount in order to maintain market share.

Sounds logical, but is it? Some companies have recognized the flaw in this type of budgeting. While the increase is justified, the amount on which it is based, the original $200,000, is not. Zero-base budgeting says that each year, instead of just adding increments to the previous year's spending, you should reexamine the entire amount. It forces the manager making the budget request to ask questions: Was this year's spending as effective as possible? Were there areas where spending could have been trimmed without hurting the marketing effort? Were there temporary conditions that called for more spending this year—such as a new product introduction–but which won't be needed next year? Have some aspects of the advertising program become outdated or ineffective? Could new tactics be used to achieve the same advertising coverage out of lower spending?

While the actual process of zero-base budgeting is beyond the scope of this manual, the possibilities that it presents for improving cash flow are such that it should be considered at least in some areas by every company. Besides examining the spending in a cost center more closely, it encourages managers to think in terms of priorities and alternatives. What is crucial in the advertising budget? What is desirable only if extra funds are available? If spending on advertising has to be cut, what alternatives to the present programs are available? How effective would they be? All of this information is extremely valuable to planners concerned with cash flow. And, of course, the zero-base technique applies to operations, engineering, research, capital spending and all other budgetary areas.

SECURITY

Security losses are one of the most severe—and most avoidable—drains on cash flow. You've already read about some of the ways you can protect inventories. Here are a few tips for plugging other security leaks:

- Insist on controls. Procedures for everyone from purchasers to accounts receivable clerks should be devised so that their actions do not go unmonitored. A good way to check the system's efficiency is to introduce deliberate errors—a short shipment, for example—and see if they are caught.
- Separate functions. The person in charge of purchasing shouldn't handle payables. Bank statements shouldn't be reconciled by the person who handles cash.
- Be suspicious. An employee never takes a vacation. A potential supplier never bids on contracts. Bad debts suddenly skyrocket. Books and records are never up-to-date. Do not take these things at face value. Demand an explanation.
- Establish accountability. Number vulnerable forms like purchase orders and invoices and make the employee who uses them accountable. Make sure that overlapping documents are checked—a shipping receipt against an invoice, for example. And have the checker sign his or her name.
- Control access. Centralize cash handling and record keeping where possible and control access to forms and books. Be especially careful to limit access to your computer if accounting functions are carried out by means of data processing.

CASH FLOW ALERT

Overspending on security can damage cash flow as much as being too lax. Make sure that the objectives of security measures (such as cutting down on shoplifting) are sufficient to cover the cost of the measures (such as the expense of installing electronic antitheft devices).

13

FINANCING CASH FLOWS

Financing generates the funds required to cover an increase in expenditures of cash. It can consist of internal financing—that is, spending the increases in the company's cash pool that are the result of profits—or external financing—obtaining additional cash in the form of new debt or equity. In either case, careful planning and analysis is necessary to ensure a smooth cash flow. The first thing managers must look at is the reasons why financing may be necessary.

SALES GROWTH

Many managers are sales-oriented. Bigger is better, they think, and sales growth is the measure of success. However, despite the fact that sales revenues are the principal source of a company's cash inflows, rapid sales growth almost always leads to cash flow problems. To see why this is so, consider the example of a successful company.

Davis Software Corporation produces a line of programs for desktop computers. A boom in the sales of these computers produced important growth opportunities for Davis. Exhibit 48 shows the cash flow projections at the company during a four-month period. Sales were

	January	February	March	April
Sales	$100,000	$110,000	$120,000	$150,000
Cash receipts	100,000	100,000	110,000	120,000
Variable costs (75% of sales)	75,000	82,500	90,000	112,500
Fixed costs	10,000	10,000	10,000	10,000
Total costs	85,000	92,500	100,000	122,500
Cash from operations	15,000	7,500	10,000	(2,500)
Accounts receivable (30 days' sales)	$100,000	$110,000	$120,000	$150,000
Inventories (30 days' sales)	100,000	110,000	120,000	150,000
Increase in accounts receivable and inventories from previous month	0	20,000	20,000	60,000
Net cash flow	$ 15,000	$(12,500)	$(10,000)	$(62,500)

Exhibit 48.
Projected cash flow, Davis Software Corporation

expected to rise 50 percent over that time. While many companies would welcome such a sales bonanza, it's apparent that Davis's managers were faced with a problem:

- Because receivables are outstanding for an average of thirty days, the sales increases do not translate into immediate gains in cash inflow.
- A total investment of $100,000, twice the amount of the monthly sales gain, is required during the period in order to finance increased receivables and inventories.
- Despite the fact that the company continues to make a gross profit of more than 15 percent of sales, it faces significant negative cash flow each month after January.

How could Davis managers handle this problem? They had four options:

1. Internal financing. The company could have amassed enough cash during the previous year and kept it in reserve in expectation of the sales increase. The managers might have delayed some discretionary capital spending in order to fill their coffers so that the needed cash would be on hand.

While internal financing is attractive—it involves no borrowing or interest payments—it is often difficult for companies in a growth situation. A sustained period of growth puts a strain on all internal sources of cash. Spending for expansion—the addition of facilities and equipment—is usually needed at this time and can't be delayed. Still, Davis was able to maintain a limited cash reserve, which helped it during the early stages of growth.

2. External financing. Bank loans and increased equity investment are another source of capital to finance growth. Unfortunately, the old adage that it's hardest to borrow money when you need it, applies here. Some lenders and investors would be put off by the projected negative cash flows and would want to restrict rather than extend financing. Davis was lucky to have established a line of credit with its bank before the sales growth began, so enough borrowing capacity was available to cover part of the cash shortfall.

3. Control working capital investment. When the cash flow shortages began to develop, Davis managers went to the company's principal suppliers and explained the situation. They stated that while they would be buying more materials and components, they would also need longer credit terms. Some of the vendors, confident that Davis was a solid and profitable firm, were willing to extend credit on payables for an extra 10, 20, or 30 days. On the receivables side, Davis began to offer a 2 percent discount to customers who paid their bills in 10 days. This brought cash in faster and cut the growth of the company's investment in receivables.

Sales growth should always be accompanied by an effort to improve cash flows. All the techniques discussed in this book for enhancing cash flow from inventories, receivables, and operations should be reviewed in order to control the amount of working capital increase.

4. Limit growth. If internal and external financing isn't available, and working capital growth is inevitable, the only alternative to a cash flow squeeze is to slow down the growth in sales. Methods for doing so range from raising prices to cutting advertising, promotions, and sales efforts. Marginal dealers and distributors can be eliminated. Less profitable product lines can be phased out. If growth in one area of your business is likely to continue for some time, you may want to sell off other product lines. This slows overall growth plus adds an influx of cash for internal financing of your main line. Always be careful, when limiting sales growth, to try to accommodate your best customers. The current demand may not last, and future cash flows depend on continued sales to principal customers.

In reality, the cash flow problems generated by sales growth are usually met by a combination of tactics. Davis managers didn't have to limit sales increases because they were able to balance the company's cash flow with a combination of internal and external financing while at the same time limiting the growth of working capital.

CASH FLOW FACTORS

Cash flow difficulties are rarely so easily solved. In many cases, sales growth is linked to other factors which have a negative influence on cash flow. Maybe a price decrease has encouraged the growth. This means lower margins, less internal cash generation, and a resulting strain on cash flow. Perhaps credit terms have been relaxed. The result is usually slower payments, increased receivables, and a higher risk of bad debts. All drain cash.

Additional sales can also be the result of an intensive advertising or promotional campaign or an increase in selling outlets. These mean higher marketing costs, an immediate drain in cash. Maybe growth stems from a new product. Development and introduction costs are incurred before a cash stream is realized for the item.

On the other hand, a decline in sales will have the opposite effect on cash flow. Not only will variable costs become less, but inventories and accounts receivable will be liquidated, bringing substantial cash inflows to the company. Other positive cash flow factors include limited introduction of new products, declining selling and promotional costs, and a low rate of inflation.

Market share can indirectly affect cash flow. The company with a high market share can usually obtain higher prices for its product while spending less on sales and promotion. The company with a low market share may have to spend more on marketing, enjoy fewer economies of sale, and be subject to price pressures from competitors. An effort to increase market share is especially burdensome to cash flow because it usually requires a combination of price cuts, promotion costs, and sales growth. Exhibit 49 lists positive and negative cash flow factors. Keep an eye on which factors are affecting each phase of your business at any one time. They may alert you to developing cash flow problems.

One of the purposes of diversification is to enter areas which balance each other on a cash flow basis. One division might be in a mature industry with slow growth and a significant market share. This type of "cash cow" will generate a positive cash flow. Another division in a young industry may need cash for new product development and marketing costs. Together, the sectors balance each other, reducing cash flow problems and limiting the need for expensive external financing.

Positive Cash Flow Factors	Negative Cash Flow Factors
Slow sales growth	Rapid sales growth
Shrinking sales	
No new product introductions	Frequent new product introductions
Declining selling costs	Increasing selling costs
Low capital intensity	High capital intensity
High market share	Low market share
Steady market share	Increasing market share
Low inflation rate	High inflation rate

Exhibit 49.
Positive and negative cash flow factors

BANK FINANCING

Your bank will almost always be your most important source of financing to alleviate cash shortages, whatever their origin. The value of maintaining good relations with a bank cannot be overemphasized because almost every company arrives at a point at which internal financing is insufficient to maintain a positive cash flow. The following points are important to remember to assure your company of an adequate supply of bank financing.

Anticipate. The middle of a cash flow crisis, when you need financing the most, is the time your banker is least likely to extend you credit. Why? First, the negative cash flow that you are facing represents a greater risk to the bank's funds. Second, the fact that you have failed to anticipate the cash shortage puts your management abilities into question.

Much better is to approach your banker six months before any problem arises and show him a carefully worked out cash budget which demonstrates that, though you will have a negative cash flow during the period, the ultimate profitability of your operation will enable you to repay the loan when it comes due. This shows planning and foresight and diminishes the banker's perceived risk. He knows he is dealing with a company which charts its course and prepares for it instead of reacting to circumstances.

CASH FLOW ALERT

Be liberal in estimating borrowing needs. Better to borrow somewhat more than you need than to have to come back to your banker later for additional funds.

Establish a line of credit. A line of credit or revolving credit agreement is particularly useful in meeting temporary cash shortages. For example, a preestablished line of credit may enable you to obtain preferred terms from suppliers. Knowing that you have the funds available when needed, they may be willing to extend to you 30- or 60-day credit instead of demanding cash. This lessens the strain on your cash flow and may not require that you borrow at all. Lines of credit are paid for by keeping a compensating balance at the bank or paying a fee.

When you do have to make use of bank financing, a revolving credit agreement—or a similar arrangement such as overdraft banking—is usually preferable to a term loan. You can obtain the cash for only the amount of time that you need to use it, pay the bank back as soon as excess cash becomes available from operations, and retain the option of drawing on credit again in the future. Much of the paperwork and delay that can accompany a term or installment loan is avoided.

CASH FLOW ALERT

Look for a bank that "fits" your company. It should be large enough to provide you with the services and credit that you need, but small enough so that you have some influence with the bank's managers.

Loyalty. Consider the customer who repeatedly runs to your competitor when he undercuts your price, but then comes back to you looking for better service. He isn't likely to be one of your valued customers. When supplies are short, he's the first one you'll cut off.

Bankers feel the same way. When credit is tight, they will meet the needs of loyal customers first. Consider this factor carefully when you're tempted to switch banks. Remember that in a cash flow crisis, it is the availability of a loan that counts most, not a minor differential in the interest rate charge. Plan your banking relationships in advance. Stay with the same bank for an extended period if you can. If you need financing or services that your regular bank can't offer, add additional sources rather than break the relationship altogether.

Keep your banker informed. This is the best way to form solid banking relationships. Inform your banker about your business and industry. What trends, cycles, customs, and changes are likely to affect your need for financing? What difficulties do you see arising in the short and long term and how do you intend to handle them? Regularly passing on basic financial and operating information to your banker will increase his knowledge and confidence in the way your firm is run.

The main thing is to avoid surprises. Give your banker the bad news along with the good. Make sure he hears about any problems from you first, not from a third party.

ALTERNATIVE FINANCING

Two reasons should prompt you to investigate alternatives to bank loans as sources of external financing. First, it's wise to have a diversity of financial sources available even if you haven't any immediate need for them. Cash flow problems and opportunities can arise quickly. Perhaps, even if your bank wishes to help you, it will be limited in the amount of loans that it can advance. Second, certain alternative sources of financing offer advantages that are not available with traditional bank loans. Some are especially useful for meeting cash flow needs.

Creative Debt and Equity

Bonds, debentures, and common and preferred stock are traditional ways of raising cash from the general investing community. Today, options in this type of financing are almost unlimited. For example, you can add the attraction of equity to a debenture by making it convertible into common stock. If you offer it at 15 percent interest, you actually pay only 9 percent after taking a tax deduction for the interest (assuming a 40 percent tax rate on your earnings). The issue, therefore, has a more attractive yield to investors than if you offered straight equity with a 9 percent dividend (which is not tax deductible). The result: you obtain financing and conserve cash at the same time.

Adjustable rate preferred stocks are another way of making an investment more attractive while limiting the burden on the company. The dividends on these issues are pegged to interest rates, making them desirable for investors, but keeping the excess debt off the books of the issuing company. Many other strategies are available. Your investment banker is the best source of advice.

You might also try to limit the cash drain represented by current financing. A stock dividend, for example, instead of a cash dividend, lets you retain cash for internal financing instead of paying it out to shareholders. A dividend reinvestment plan—used successfully by many U.S. companies today—cycles cash paid in dividends back into the company. It provides a convenient and steady source of additional cash flow.

CASH FLOW ALERT

It can often be profitable to look for cash outside your home country. If you can't find medium or long-term credit sources domestically, foreign borrowing may fill your needs. Loan brokers can help you to find money which may carry a lower interest rate than that charged by local banks. If you do business in that country, the loan can also serve as a foreign exchange hedge.

Hidden Assets

Where does your company turn if it does not wish to go to the financial markets, has reached the limit of its bank financing, and needs cash quickly to stem an expected cash shortage? One solution is to acquire cash through your company's own assets. Especially after a time of inflation, the book value of a company's equipment and facilities is often far below the replacement or liquidation value of the property. All that is needed to turn this value into cash is to contact a commercial lender who specializes in that type of financing.

Companies who traditionally borrow from banks may not be aware of the possibilities of secured lending. Banks are usually reluctant to loan on the basis of pledged assets because they have neither the ability to evaluate the worth of the collateral, nor the facilities to liquidate it, should the borrower default. Commercial lenders have both.

CASH FLOW ALERT

Even your inventories may be the source of quick cash through commercial financing. Check with companies that specialize in this type of financing. They may be willing to lend you a large portion of the value of inventories in exchange for a lien on them.

One version of this type of lending is what is known as a cash conservation loan. For example, a printing company wants to increase its capacity by adding a new press costing $200,000. But the purchase requires a down payment of 20 percent, or $40,000. The company can't afford that much immediate cash outflow.

However, the company's current press, even though depreciation has reduced its book value to a mere $10,000, could actually be sold on the secondhand market for at least $60,000. A commercial finance company will be willing to lend the company the $40,000 and take a lien on the old press. Therefore, the firm can achieve 100 percent financing on the new press, purchasing it with no immediate outflow of cash.

Two myths exist about secured lending. One is that it is financing "of last resort" and that only companies on the verge of bankruptcy pledge their assets as collateral. This is not true. Though secured lending may be more expensive than bank loans, it offers numerous advantages to any company in terms of flexibility, diversification of credit sources, and manipulation of cash flow.

The other myth is that your company's primary banker will frown on your using assets as collateral when you are currently in debt to the bank. This is not so under normal conditions. Your banker is backing your company as a going business, not because of its liquidation value. He would rather see you obtain the working capital you need to increase your ultimate profitability than have you maintain clear title to your equipment but fail to operate in a viable fashion.

CASH FLOW ALERT

Instead of extending credit to customers or forcing them to find their own financing, you can arrange with a commercial finance company to underwrite the financing of your products. The finance company will undertake credit and collection responsibilities. Your product will be easier to sell and your cash flow will improve. This is particularly true for makers of capital equipment.

FACTORING

Receivables-based financing, or factoring, was once confined to a few industries. Today, as banks have joined specialty factoring firms, it has grown to a popular form of financing for a wide range of smaller and medium-sized companies. Almost any company with a diversified customer base, a large number of customers, average invoices over $300, and credit terms ranging from 30 to 90 days may have some use for factoring.

Normally, a factor takes over the company's credit reporting and collection efforts and perhaps its bookkeeping for accounts receivable. The company receives payment from the factor as soon as the sales are made, minus a fee ranging from ¾ to 2 percent of the face amount. It also pays interest on the cash advance up until the maturity of the related receivables. Factoring puts cash in the company's hand immediately following the sale rather than after a delay, and it can relieve the firm of the cost of tracking and collecting accounts. It can give you the funds, for example, to take advantage of discounts offered by suppliers for paying your bills early. Some of the uses of factoring are:

Growth. As discussed above, sales growth often strains cash resources. Factoring allows cash receipts to keep pace with sales levels instead of lagging two, three, or more months behind.

Seasonal needs. Factoring is a traditional tool for companies whose revenues fluctuate widely through a year. It increases their cash reserves at the time when they are needed to finance production in anticipation of the selling season, and then allows them to realize cash from sales quickly so that they can pay their bills. Some companies even take advantage of over–advance factoring. In that case, the factoring company advances cash not only on current receivables but also on anticipated receivables. This provides an extra inflow of cash when it is needed.

Flexibility. Factoring companies have substantial resources and excellent credit verification facilities. Therefore, they can often provide more liberal credit than you can, taking on the accounts of customers that you would find too risky if you had to assume the liability for their accounts. Quick approval of credit can speed sales to new customers, too.

International. Factoring can be very helpful in international trade, where receipt of cash is often very slow. One type of factoring, called au forfaiting, involves having a customer pay you with a debt instrument, such as a promissory note. You present this to a lender, who gives you an appropriately discounted amount of cash and takes over the responsibility of collecting the amount when due.

CASH FLOW ALERT

You can turn a factor's backing into a letter of credit which will allow you to expedite additional foreign contracts without immediate cash spending.

14

HOW TO CONSERVE CASH THROUGH LEASING

The lease or buy decision is not a capital spending decision. That is, you are not deciding whether to make an investment, but how to finance an investment. You have already determined that a piece of equipment, a vehicle, or a facility is a worthwhile expenditure. Now you are trying to determine whether to buy the item outright—either using internal funds or borrowed money—or to lease it.

Leasing has important cash flow implications and should be considered whenever your company faces significant expenditures. Usually, leasing applies to property with a minimum useful life of three years. It does not often apply to property whose use could not be transferred to another party. For example, while a truck could be leased, pipes installed in a processing plant could not be.

From a cash flow perspective, the important thing is to keep in mind the lease option. Leasing can provide creative solutions to cash problems as well as improve day-to-day cash flow. Before considering how to analyze the lease/buy decision, consider a few of the advantages and disadvantages of leasing and look at the accompanying cash flow effects.

Advantages of Leasing

Lower initial payment. Leasing requires minimal up-front outflow of cash compared to the down payment and other costs that accompany a purchase.

Smaller payments. Both banks and commercial finance companies are reluctant to extend credit for more than 4 or 5 years. A lease can run up to 7 or 10 years, meaning that each payment is substantially smaller.

Affordability. Given your company's current cash and credit situation, it may not be able to either buy the equipment outright or obtain the needed financing. Leasing allows you to take possession of the item and begin using it now. Waiting until it becomes affordable may allow profit opportunities to slip by.

Stability. Leasing usually locks in a set payment schedule over the life of the lease. Loans to finance purchases are often linked to interest rate fluctuations. The cost of capital over the life of a lease is a known quantity.

Cash Flow Effect

Conserves cash, reduces the need for an immediate cash outflow.

Conserves cash in the near term and puts off payments until a time in the future when cash may be more plentiful.

The company achieves the cash flow benefits that can be obtained from the property at once rather than having to wait.

Facilitates cash projections, cash forecasting, and cash planning.

Advantages of Leasing

Leasing does not deplete available credit, which would have to be drawn on to finance a purchase if the company didn't have a large cash reserve.

Leasing results in diversification of financing. In a sense, leasing uses the lessor as a source of financing, avoiding the company's dependence on a single bank or other lender.

Modernization. Leases—called upgrade leases—can be arranged which allow for substitution of new and improved models of the equipment as they become available. The lessor's access to markets for used equipment facilitates his disposal of the old item. Selling it after a purchase may be more difficult.

Service. Leasing usually automatically includes service by the lessor. While purchasing can be accompanied by service contracts, these are sometimes not economical. Service allows the lessee to avoid many maintenance problems, as well as the expense of stocking maintenance inventories.

Cash Flow Effect

Gives the company more flexibility to raise cash in the future in the event that special needs arise.

Increases total sources of cash available.

Prevents the resulting drain on cash flow if the company has to sell the equipment and purchase a new model.

Eliminates unexpected maintenance costs and lowers inventory carrying expenses. Enhances cash flow reliability.

Advantages of Leasing

Reliability. If the equipment malfunctions or does not perform as expected, the lessor may have to correct the situation. It may be harder to get the manufacturer to take action if the equipment is purchased.

Purchase option. If your company arranges a lease with an option to purchase the equipment in the future, then the decision to purchase can be made after you have had practical experience with the equipment.

Inflation hedge. Leasing provides two benefits in times of high inflation. First, you obtain the advantages of the equipment now rather than waiting until the price is even higher in order to purchase. Second, you can lease at today's prices and pay back in inflated money in the future.

Tax benefits. While tax advantages can be obtained in both purchase and lease arrangements, companies which are capital intensive often can't use the credits and depreciation that

Cash Flow Effect

Lessee stands less of a risk to cash flows if equipment malfunctions.

More information on actual cash flow advantages are available before final decision to purchase. Reduces risk.

A reduction in the ultimate real cost of the equipment.

Lowers the overall cost of the equipment.

Advantages of Leasing (cont.)

flow from an outright purchase. The lessor can use those advantages and pass on savings to the lessee.

Disadvantages of Leasing

Cost. In most cases, the overall cost of leasing will be greater than that of purchasing. The lessor is a middleman between you and the manufacturer. He is in business to make a profit, and his profit comes from the excess of lease payments over the base cost of the equipment.

Revocability. Perhaps the equipment does not produce the results or cash flow you expected. Maybe you abandon the project with which it is connected. If you own the item, you can sell it. If you lease, you are often obligated to pay many more installments and cannot easily revoke the lease.

Loss of equipment. If your lease does not contain a renewal clause, the lessor could take back the equipment at the end of the lease, leaving you without its use.

Cash Flow Effect

The total long-term drain on cash flow from leased equipment is usually higher than that resulting from a purchase.

You risk substantial cash flow drain from the remaining lease payments if the project has to be discontinued.

Your cash flow could be impeded as you search for new equipment to buy or lease.

Disadvantages of Leasing

Loss of residual value. The value of the equipment at the end of the lease can be substantial, especially in times of inflation when the replacement cost has steadily mounted over the lease period. If you purchase, this value can lessen the financial impact of the transaction. If you lease, the benefit usually goes to the lessor.

Tax benefits. If your company has substantial earnings and pays a high rate of tax, it could probably benefit from tax incentives and accelerated depreciation charges connected with purchases. While lease payments can be deducted as expenses, they have a much lesser effect on cash flow and are spread out longer.

Cash Flow Effect

This further increases the overall drain on cash flow compared with purchasing. It eliminates a possible cash inflow at the time you dispose of the equipment.

High early tax deductions from purchasing partly offset the drain on cash flow represented by the initial payments.

DECIDING WHETHER TO LEASE

The decision whether to lease or purchase a piece of equipment will be based on a number of factors. Financial elements will be paramount, but such aspects as convenience, flexibility, and diversification of credit sources should also be taken into account.

Leases are generally classified in two categories. Capital leases are actually long-term financial arrangements that closely resemble purchases and are treated as such in the U.S. for accounting purposes. Operating leases are true leases in which the lessee pays only for the use of the equipment. All lease or buy decisions are based on a comparison of an operating lease with a purchase.

CASH FLOW ALERT

Some companies lease to present a healthier balance sheet to investors and potential lenders. Operating leases do not show up as a liability or weaken debt/equity ratios. As a result, the company may find it easier to raise needed cash.

Tax benefits usually play a large role in lease-or-buy decisions. To begin with, because both lease payments and interest charges on loans are tax deductible, actual costs must be calculated after taxes. Secondly, depreciation and tax benefits like the investment tax credit apply to purchased goods and must be calculated into the equation in order to arrive at true costs.

Because of the complicated nature of the calculations involved, formal, detailed analysis of the financial side of the lease-or-buy decision should be made in the financial department. However, operating managers should have a general view of the factors that affect leasing in order to spot leasing opportunities that can contribute to cash flow. The following example will illustrate a typical analysis.

THE ECONOMICS OF THE LEASE-OR-BUY DECISION

A plant manager at Wilson Manufacturing Co. decided that if the company had its own truck for making local deliveries, it could save money and generate new business. A capital spending analysis verified that the action would represent a good use of funds. Now the manager wanted to decide whether to recommend leasing or buying the truck.

CASH FLOW ALERT

Up-front costs to purchase, usually avoided by leasing, include sales tax and loan origination fees in addition to a down payment. All require immediate cash outflow and shouldn't be neglected in making your decision.

To purchase the truck, the company would have to pay $50,000 in the form of a $10,000 down payment and a $40,000 bank loan at 13 percent interest over four years. Since the interest on the loan would be deductible, the manager found the savings in taxes by multiplying the interest payments by the company's tax rate of 46 percent. He did the same for the depreciation resulting from purchasing the asset, since that too would lower taxes.

He subtracted the investment tax credit that the company would receive if it purchased, since that would directly lower taxes.

Since he figured the company would want a service contract for the truck, he added the after-tax cost of that ($300/quarter). Once he found the quarterly cost of the purchase, he multiplied each amount after the initial payment by a 4 percent present value factor, which represented the company's 16 percent hurdle rate for the cost of capital. His calculations are shown in Exhibit 50.

To lease the truck, the company would have to pay $3,400 per quarter over four years. Since this payment is tax deductible, the manager calculated the after-tax cost, which amounted to $1,836 per quarter ($3,400 × 0.54). He calculated the present value of each quarter's payments and added them to find the total present value of the lease. These calculations are shown in Exhibit 51.

Quarter	Total Payment (Including Service Charge)	Tax Savings* (Including Interest, Depreciation, and $3,500 Investment Tax Credit)	Net Cost	Present Value Factor (@ 4%)	Present Value
0	$10,000	$3,500	$ 6,500	1.000	$ 6,500
1	3,546	2,898	648	.962	623
2	3,546	2,869	677	.925	626
3	3,546	2,839	707	.889	629
4	3,546	2,808	738	.855	631
5	3,546	2,201	1,345	.822	1,106
6	3,546	2,168	1,378	.790	1,089
7	3,546	2,133	1,413	.760	1,074
8	3,546	2,099	1,447	.731	1,058
9	3,546	1,487	2,059	.703	1,448
10	3,546	1,449	2,097	.676	1,418
11	3,546	1,411	2,135	.650	1,388
12	3,546	1,370	2,176	.625	1,360
13	3,546	754	2,792	.601	1,678
14	3,546	712	2,834	.578	1,638
15	3,546	667	2,879	.555	1,598
16	3,546	625	2,921	.534	1,560
		Total	$34,746		$25,424

*Note: Tax savings represent the company's 46% tax rate and sum-of-the-years digits depreciation method.

Exhibit 50.
The cost of the purchase option

What the manager discovered was that the present value of the cost of purchasing was slightly more than $2,000 greater than the cost of leasing. Other factors being equal, this would make the manager choose leasing as the less costly alternative.

Cash Flow Effects

In addition to the total present value of each option, the manager was interested in the timing of cash expenditures represented by leasing or purchasing. The following figures show the cumulative after-tax cash outflows required by each approach:

Quarter	Lease	Buy
0	$ 1,836	$ 6,500
1	3,672	7,148
2	5,508	7,825

Quarter	Lease Cost After Taxes	Present Value Factor (@ 4%)	Present Value
0	$ 1,836	1.000	$ 1,836
1	1,836	.962	1,766
2	1,836	.925	1,698
3	1,836	.889	1,632
4	1,836	.855	1,570
5	1,836	.822	1,509
6	1,836	.790	1,450
7	1,836	.760	1,395
8	1,836	.731	1,342
9	1,836	.703	1,291
10	1,836	.676	1,241
11	1,836	.650	1,193
12	1,836	.625	1,148
13	1,836	.601	1,103
14	1,836	.578	1,061
15	1,836	.555	1,019
16	1,836	.534	980
Total	$29,376		$23,234

Exhibit 51.
The cost of the lease option

Quarter	Lease	Buy
3	7,344	8,532
4	9,180	9,270
5	11,016	10,615
6	12,852	11,993

The manager noted that during the entire first year, leasing requires less cash expenditure than does purchasing. This could be an important factor in the lease-or-buy decision. Perhaps his company is short of cash. The use of the new truck is expected to increase profits, improving the cash position by next year. In that case, Wilson Manufacturing will be even more inclined to lease in order to put off payments until a time when cash inflows are greater.

Other Factors

But the residual value of the truck is another important issue. After four years it may still be relatively high. If Wilson purchases it, the company will be able to make use of this value, perhaps as a trade-in on a new truck. The leasing option assigns the residual value to the leasing company, leaving Wilson with nothing when the lease expires. The manager has to decide whether this factor is more significant than the financial advantages of leasing.

Also, purchasing gives Wilson the advantage of selling the truck when it wishes. Maybe local sales will decline and the firm will no longer need the truck. If it leases it, the firm will still be liable for the payments. With a purchase, it has a good chance of recovering the cash through a sale.

On the other hand, maybe the availability of the truck will result in greatly expanded business. The company may want to obtain another truck or enlarge its facilities. If, by purchasing, it has used up cash on the down payment and depleted its credit with the bank loan, it may not be in a position to raise the needed funds quickly. Leasing conserves cash and leaves lines of credit available.

The decision, then, is not an easy one. Only after a full analysis of all these factors, will the manager be able to recommend whether it is better to lease or buy the truck.

> **CASH FLOW ALERT**
>
> Conserving credit is a strong argument for leasing. Once you have borrowed money to purchase an item, you have diminished possible sources of credit that may be needed for working capital emergencies. Leasing keeps your options open.

Negotiations

This example assumes that Wilson Manufacturing was faced with fixed terms from the leasing company it had chosen. In practice, most lessors are willing to extend some flexibility to help accommodate the lessee's individual needs. For example, a large part of Wilson's sales occurred in the autumn. The leasing company might be willing to structure lease payments which were lower in the spring and summer and higher in the autumn and winter. Perhaps it would be willing to extend the period of the lease, enabling Wilson to improve near-term cash flow through smaller payments. Maybe a purchase option could be included, allowing the company to take advantage of the residual value or some part of it.

After you have made a detailed lease-or-buy analysis, go back to the leasing company and try to negotiate better terms before making the final decision. The company may be willing to arrange payments that will make the lease option more advantageous.

> **CASH FLOW ALERT**
>
> The leasing option does not necessarily require you to take on new equipment. Sale and lease-back arrangements can provide cash flow benefits on existing property. Current equipment or facilities are sold to investors and then leased under long-term contracts, giving the company an immediate infusion of cash.

APPENDIX

TABLE OF PRESENT VALUE FACTORS

Periods	1%	2%	4%	6%	8%	10%	12%	14%
1	.990	.980	.962	.943	.926	.909	.893	.877
2	.980	.961	.925	.890	.857	.826	.797	.769
3	.971	.942	.889	.840	.794	.751	.712	.675
4	.961	.924	.855	.792	.735	.683	.636	.592
5	.951	.906	.822	.747	.681	.621	.567	.519
6	.942	.888	.790	.705	.630	.564	.507	.456
7	.933	.871	.760	.665	.583	.513	.452	.400
8	.923	.853	.731	.627	.540	.467	.404	.351
9	.914	.837	.703	.592	.500	.424	.361	.308
10	.905	.820	.676	.558	.463	.386	.322	.270
11	.896	.804	.650	.527	.429	.350	.287	.237
12	.887	.788	.625	.497	.397	.319	.257	.208
13	.879	.773	.601	.469	.368	.290	.229	.182
14	.870	.758	.578	.442	.340	.263	.205	.160

TABLE OF PRESENT VALUE FACTORS (Continued)

Periods	1%	2%	4%	6%	8%	10%	12%	14%
15	.861	.743	.555	.417	.315	.239	.183	.140
16	.853	.728	.534	.394	.292	.218	.163	.123
17	.844	.714	.513	.371	.270	.198	.146	.108
18	.836	.700	.494	.350	.250	.180	.130	.095
19	.828	.686	.475	.331	.232	.164	.116	.083
20	.820	.673	.456	.312	.215	.149	.104	.073
21	.811	.660	.439	.294	.199	.135	.093	.064
22	.803	.647	.422	.278	.184	.123	.083	.056
23	.795	.634	.406	.262	.170	.112	.074	.049
24	.788	.622	.390	.247	.158	.102	.066	.043
25	.780	.610	.375	.233	.146	.092	.059	.038
26	.772	.598	.361	.220	.135	.084	.053	.033
27	.764	.586	.347	.207	.125	.076	.047	.029
28	.757	.574	.333	.196	.116	.069	.042	.026
29	.749	.563	.321	.185	.107	.063	.037	.022
30	.742	.552	.308	.174	.099	.057	.033	.020

Periods	15%	16%	18%	20%	22%	24%	25%	26%
1	.870	.862	.847	.833	.820	.806	.800	.794
2	.756	.743	.718	.694	.672	.650	.640	.630
3	.658	.641	.609	.579	.551	.524	.512	.500
4	.572	.552	.516	.482	.451	.423	.410	.397
5	.497	.476	.437	.402	.370	.341	.328	.315
6	.432	.410	.370	.335	.303	.275	.262	.250
7	.376	.354	.314	.279	.249	.222	.210	.198
8	.327	.305	.266	.233	.204	.179	.168	.157
9	.284	.263	.225	.194	.167	.144	.134	.125
10	.247	.227	.191	.162	.137	.116	.107	.099

TABLE OF PRESENT VALUE FACTORS (Continued)

Periods	15%	16%	18%	20%	22%	24%	25%	26%
11	.215	.195	.162	.135	.112	.094	.086	.079
12	.187	.168	.137	.112	.092	.076	.069	.062
13	.163	.145	.116	.093	.075	.061	.055	.050
14	.141	.125	.099	.078	.062	.049	.044	.039
15	.123	.108	.084	.065	.051	.040	.035	.031
16	.107	.093	.071	.054	.042	.032	.028	.025
17	.093	.080	.060	.045	.034	.026	.023	.020
18	.081	.069	.051	.038	.028	.021	.018	.016
19	.070	.060	.043	.031	.023	.017	.014	.012
20	.061	.051	.037	.026	.019	.014	.012	.010
21	.053	.044	.031	.022	.015	.011	.009	.008
22	.046	.038	.026	.018	.013	.009	.007	.006
23	.040	.033	.022	.015	.010	.007	.006	.005
24	.035	.028	.019	.013	.008	.006	.005	.004
25	.030	.024	.016	.010	.007	.005	.004	.003
26	.026	.021	.014	.009	.006	.004	.003	.002
27	.023	.018	.011	.007	.005	.003	.002	.002
28	.020	.016	.010	.006	.004	.002	.002	.002
29	.017	.014	.008	.005	.003	.002	.002	.001
30	.015	.012	.007	.004	.003	.002	.001	.001

Periods	28%	30%	35%	40%	45%	50%
1	.781	.769	.741	.714	.690	.667
2	.610	.592	.549	.510	.476	.444
3	.477	.455	.406	.364	.328	.296
4	.373	.350	.301	.260	.226	.198
5	.291	.269	.223	.186	.156	.132
6	.227	.207	.165	.133	.108	.088

TABLE OF PRESENT VALUE FACTORS (Continued)

Periods	28%	30%	35%	40%	45%	50%
7	.178	.159	.122	.095	.074	.059
8	.139	.123	.091	.068	.051	.039
9	.108	.094	.067	.048	.035	.026
10	.085	.073	.050	.035	.024	.017
11	.066	.056	.037	.025	.017	.012
12	.052	.043	.027	.018	.012	.008
13	.040	.033	.020	.013	.008	.005
14	.032	.025	.015	.009	.006	.003
15	.025	.020	.011	.006	.004	.002
16	.019	.015	.008	.005	.003	.002
17	.015	.012	.006	.003	.002	.001
18	.012	.009	.005	.002	.001	.001
19	.009	.007	.003	.002	.001	
20	.007	.005	.002	.001	.001	
21	.006	.004	.002	.001		
22	.004	.003	.001	.001		
23	.003	.002	.001			
24	.003	.002	.001			
25	.002	.001	.001			
26	.002	.001				
27	.001	.001				
28	.001	.001				
29	.001	.001				
30	.001					

INDEX

ABC analysis of inventories, 15–18, 30
Accelerated depreciation, 135
Accounting, 167–168; for inventories, 47–51
Accounts receivable, 4, 5; aging, 76–80, 83; controlling, 71–82; DDO analysis of, 83–89; DSO analysis of, 74–76, 80, 83; effect on cash flow, 72–73, 87–95; weighted analysis of, 83–95
Advertising, 144
Aging analyses, 76–80, 83
Airlines, 170
Alternative financing, 186–189
Asset, cash as an, 6–7
Audits, 171
Auto industry, 157, 173

Bad debts, 77, 81, 98, 99, 101, 109, 113–119
Bailout factor, 133–134
Bank financing, 184–186, 188, 189
Bankruptcy, 7, 8, 114
Bonds, 186
Break-even analysis for volume discounts, 57–70

Capital leases, 196–197
Capital spending and cash flow, 129–150; creative approaches to, 147–148; identifying and evaluating projects, 144–147; risk in, 141–144
Carrying costs of inventory, 18–21, 30, 32, 34, 37, 38
Cash consciousness, 8–10

Cash flow effect: of collection efforts, 87–95; of credit decisions, 99–100, 105–111, 113–118
Cash flow factors, 182–183
Cash flow range, 141–142
Catalogs, 168
Central records office, 175
Clerical costs, 174–175
Communications, 158, 166, 174
Competition, 105
Conservation, 162
Cost of capital, 19
Creative debt, 186–187
Credit evaluation reports, 125–128
Credit managers, 10, 100, 101, 105
Credit policy, 71–82, 97–111; cash flow effect of, 99–100, 105–111, 113–118; and evaluation of customers, 113–128; and profit margins, 119–121; risk situations, 102, 103–104, 113–115, 122–125; terms, 105–111
Customer accounts, analyzing, 80–82
Customers, evaluation of, 113–128

Damage, inventory, 21
Days of inventory on hand, 42–44
Days Sales Outstanding (DSO) analysis, 74–76, 80, 83
Definition of cash flow, 4–5

Depreciation, 4–5, 134–137; purchase volume, cash flow analysis of, 55–70
Disposing of excess inventory, 44–45
Dollar Days Outstanding (DDO) analysis, 83–89
Double-declining balance (DDB), 135

Economic order quantity (EOQ) analysis, 29–40
Efficiency, production, 153–157
Employee relations, 172–173
Employee theft, 51–54
Energy conservation, 162
Engineering, 155
Equity, 186–187
Evaluation of customers, 113–128
Excess inventory, 41–47
External financing, 179, 181, 184–187

Factoring, 189–190
Financing cash flows, 179–190
First in, first out (FIFO), 50
Forms, 175–176
Fuel, 145
Future operating costs, estimates of, 142

General Electric Co., 162, 166
General Motors, 157
Giveaways, 170–171
Grant & Co (W.T.), 7

Handling of inventory, 20

Health care costs, 173
Hidden assets, 187–189

Inflation, 50, 183, 194
Inspections, 53
Insurance, 171–172, 173; inventory, 20, 21
Interest rates, 6, 19, 187
Internal financing, 179, 181, 187–189
Internal rate of return (IRR), 139–140
Inventories, 4, 5–6, 11–54, 60, 99, 106, 109, 156, 157, 188; ABC analysis of, 15–18, 30; accounting for, 47–51; boom-and-bust policy, 39–40; bottlenecks in, 148; control and reduction techniques, 29–40; costs of carrying, 18–21, 30, 32, 34, 37, 38; EOQ analysis of, 29–40; measuring turnover, 21–22, 23, 25, 26; obsolete and excess, handling of, 41–47; and quality control, 160–161; return on investment, 23–27; reviews of, 15; right level of, 12–15; security losses, 51–54
Investment tax credit, 135

Japan, 152, 157
Joint ventures, 147
Just-in-Time (JIT) method of production scheduling, 157

Labor costs, 151, 156, 173

Last in, first out (LIFO), 50, 51
Leasing, 191–202
Legal costs, 169–170

Machinery, 145, 151–159
Maintenance, 144, 146, 174
Make/buy decision, 164–166
Market, 145, 183
Materials, 145, 157–166; and quality control, 160–161; shortages, 166
Materials requirement planning (MRP), 45–47, 48
Modernization, 144, 193
Months-of-inventory-on-hand ratio, 41

Net present value analysis (NPV), 136–138, 139

Obsolete and excess inventory, 20, 21, 41–47
Oil industry, 7–8
Operating leases, 197
Operation and procedure improvements to conserve cash, 167–178
Ordering costs and problems, 29–40

Parts numbers, 47
Payback period analysis, 129–133
Plant layout and safety, 156–157
Present value index, 138
Production: efficiency, 153–157; improving cash flow in, 151–166; managers, 10, 29, 146,

Production (*continued*):
152, 158; and quality control, 160–161; scheduling, 157–159; setup schedules, 152–153
Product mix, 118–121
Profit margins and credit policy, 119–121
Purchase volume discounts, cash flow analysis of, 55–70
Purchasing managers, 10, 37, 38, 55, 57, 60–61, 66–67, 166

Quality control, 160–61

Receiving manager, 163
Research and development projects, 144
Reviews, inventory, 15
Risk: -adjusted discounting, 142–143; in capital projects, 141–144; classification system, 124–125

Sales forecasts, 111
Sales growth, 179–182, 190
Scheduling production, 157–159
Scrap, 145, 159–160
Security losses, 51–54, 177–178
Self-insurance, 172
Selling costs, 168–169
Sensitivity analysis, 143–144
Setup schedules, 152–513
Shipping, 162–163, 170, 171
Shrinkage, inventory, 20
Standardization, 154–156
Stocks, 186–187

Storage of inventory, 20, 21
Straight-line depreciation, 135
Sum-of-the-years digits (SYD), 135

Tax(es), 44, 50, 186; benefits, and leasing, 194–200; and depreciation, 135–136
Telephone costs, 174
Theft, inventory, 51–54
Timing: of cash flows on credit decisions, 115–118; and volume discounts, 60–61
Trade receivables, 71
Turnover, inventory, 21–22, 23, 25, 26
20/80 rule, 16

Used equipment, 147

Value analysis (VA), 163–164
Vendors, 160
Volume discounts, cash flow analysis of, 55–70

Warehouse, 151; security, 52–53; storage, 20, 21
Weighted analysis for cash flow improvement, 83-95
Westinghouse Electric Corporation, 163
Working capital investment, control of, 181
Write-offs, 44

Zero-base budgeting, 176–177